HIGHER EDUCATION THROUGH TELEVISION

About the Editor

Binod C. Agrawal (Ph. D. Wisconsin) currently Director, TALEEM Research Foundation is involved in promoting open and distance learning and setting up University on the Sky. Until recently he was Advisor to the Space Applications Centre (ISRO), Ahemedabad. Dr. Agrawal has been associated with satellite communication applications programme since 1975-76, when the world-famous tech-social Satellite Instructional Television Experiment (SITE) was carried out in India. He was responsible for the social evaluation of the SITE and later published Social Evaluation: Results, Experiences and Implications (1981). In the recent past, his area of interest has been computer technology and education. Another area in which Dr. Agrawal has been deeply involved, is use of satellite communication for distance education and teleconferencing.

Dr. Agrawal was the first Director, Mudra institute of Communications. Ahmedabad (MICA).

Currently, he is President, National Council of Development Communication, and involved with various international research projects. His publications include over a dozen books on the use of communication for development and education. His articles are published frequently in various national and international research journals.

HIGHER EDUCATION THROUGH TELEVISION

The Indian Experience

Edited by
Binod C. Agrawal

CONCEPT PUBLISHING COMPANY PVT. LTD.
NEW DELHI-110059

ISBN : 978-81-7022-809-7

Edition 2020

Published and Printed by

Concept
Since 1974

Concept Publishing Company Pvt. Ltd.
A/15-16, Commercial Block, Mohan Garden,
New Delhi-110059 (INDIA)
T: +91 11 25351460, +91 11 25351794
E: publishing@conceptpub.com, *W*: www.conceptpub.com

Cataloging in Publication Data--Courtesy: D.K. Agencies (P) Ltd. <docinfo@dkagencies.com>

Higher education through television : the Indian experience / edited by Binod C. Agrawal.
pages cm
Reprint. Originally published: 2000.
Includes bibliographical references and index.
ISBN 9788170228097

1. Television in higher education--India. 2. Education, Higher--India. 3. Distance education--India. I. Agrawal, Binod C., 1942- editor.

LCC LB1044.7.H54 2020 | DDC 378.173580954 23

INTRODUCTION

In this volume the author has brought together his earlier writings on media and education after the arrival of INSAT for nationwide broadcasting. INSAT brought a communication revolution in the broadcasting scenario of India. Since 1982 there has been a remarkable expansion of television. Privatization without sanction popularly known as invasion from the sky in early 90's has changed the television scenario in India from a single channel nation to a multi-channel country having over 50 channels all across. While there has been a tremendous expansion in the field of television very little has been done for the expansion of television for education.

The papers included in this volume reflect the earlier thought on the use of television for education that are still relevant in the contemporary context of India. These papers cover theoretical discussions on the structural predicaments in providing education to all in India through any mode or medium. Other papers in the volume present empirical researches in the use of television for higher education and contemporary uses in the utilization of television for education especially in the broadcasting mode. The author has also discussed communication researches related to television in India.

The common theme that runs throughout this book is that education *per se* whether in the ancient times or in the contemporary context, was and remains a victim of the very social structure in which it flourished. From all accounts education benefits the rich. The second theme supported by research is that television use can help bridge the educational gap between students of elite and non-elite colleges.

Fast changing communication technology scenario has not reduced the importance of television for education, on the contrary it has helped strengthen an appropriate use of television for education in a multimedia context which is fast growing in India. This book therefore must be read by students both of communication and education.

BINOD C. AGRAWAL

ACKNOWLEDGEMENTS

I am grateful to all those institutions and organisations who directly or indirectly helped me in writing eight paper included in this volume. I am especially grateful to UN University, Tokyo for assistance in writing the first paper. The fourth and fifth papers are research studies conducted with the support provided by University Grants Commission. The detailed reference of each paper is given below :

1. "Culture, Communication and Knowledge : The Structural Predicaments", an unpublished paper written under the IOIO Project of UN University, Tokyo, Japan (1986).
2. "Culture and Communication Technology in the Indian Higher Education : A Synergy or a Mismatch", jointly written with N. Kalayanaraman. *In New Technologies in Higher Education* edited by S.Y. Shah, New Delhi : Association of Indian Universities 1986.
3. "Education and Socio-Cultural Implications of Satellite Communication : Some Observations", written for UNESCO International Seminar on the "Application of Communication Technology in Education among Developing Countries" held at University Kebangsaan, Malaysia on December 7-8, 1987.
4. "INSAT Pre-Production (Formative) Television Research for Countrywide Classroom" is a modified version of the first part of the report, *INSAT Pre-Production Television Research for Higher Education : A Consolidated Report for UGC.* Compiled and edited in collaboration with Mira B. Aghi and Arundhati Ramanathan (1986).
5. "Message System Analysis of UGC Countrywide Classroom" is an UGC sponsored study conducted in collaboration with J.N. Hashmi, Imtiaz Kar, Arbind Sinha and Jyotsna Verma of Development and Educational Communication Unit, Ahmedabad March 1, 1988.
6. "Educational Impact of Distance Learning : An Evaluation of Tele-Symposium via APPLE on Satellite Communications" is a modified report prepared in September 1983 for Educational Resources Cell, Space Applications Centre, Ahmedabad.

7. "Video Use in Distance Education : A South Asian Perspective" is an unpublished paper presented in CIDA-AMIC seminar on "Training Needs in the Use of Media for Distance Education in Asia", held at the Asian Mass Communication Research and Information Centre, Singapore from June 8-11, 1987 (now in press).
8. "Television Studies in India : The State of the Art" is an unpublished paper presented in the International Television Studies Conferences, held at London, UK, in July 1986.

I am thankful to my co-authors and especially Jyotsna Verma who helped in giving shape to this book. I am also thankful to Kalpana Rao who edited and proof read the volume. Last but not the least I am grateful to Omana Raghavan who typed the manuscript and Priya Raghavan for giving the final shape to the book.

Ahmedabad
August 1, 1999

BINOD C. AGRAWAL

CONTENTS

LIST OF FIGURES

LIST OF FIGURES

1

CULTURE, COMMUNICATION AND KNOWLEDGE

The Structural Predicaments

BINOD C. AGRAWAL

THERE IS a great deal of talk about 'communication revolution' and 'emerging information societies' as a result of large scale expansion of information technology and the communication media in North America, Europe and Japan. It is assumed that a similar revolution and type of society will inevitably evolve in the Afro-Asian countries as a result of ongoing media explosion. However, there are differing perceptions of these concepts of a communication revolution and information society, especially in Asia. No culture or society survives without information and all living cultures or civilisations are 'information societies' in one form or the other. They have their own methods of information processing, knowledge generation and transfer.

Information must be generated in persuasive forms to be accepted by the generation receiving it as its repertoire of values, beliefs and ethos. It forms the basis of a knowledge system which grows and will be modified, or may be, even degenerate, leading to the eventual extinction of the culture. It is through this process of information generation, processing, knowledge creation and transfer and in this context that I would talk of an information society.

The issues of communication, cultural regeneration and survival need to be discussed seriously and elaborated in the context of any notion of 'communication revolution' and 'emerging information societies'. What is the method by which accumulated knowledge is transferred to the next generation? How does change occur in existing knowledge and information leading to change within a given culture? Does increased communication capability improve and enhance the capacity for sharing and exchange? And would that by itself lead to an 'information society'? or a 'communication revolution'. It is the contention of this paper that it will not.

In the context of Asian civilizations, the notion of a communication revolution is a debatable one. Any culture which has an inbuilt heirarchy, in terms of economic class and social systems, will not allow all its members to reap the fruits of communication technologies. It may be mentioned in passing that while there is an attempt at increased information sharing, both at the global and individual cultural levels, there are also serious efforts to withhold and suppress information of all kinds; and this, often in the large political, economic and national interest.

In Asia, it is the structural inhibitions which would negate the possibility of any such revolution. The technology of communication might be available to these cultures, but a revolution of mass participation will not arise. The technology will not percolate to all those who should, or desire to, share it. Instead, it will remain confined to a small group of cultural elite. And the change, if any, will be a means of learning, knowledge and power gain for this minority, and a new tool for increased exploitation of the majority.

The paper aims to elaborate the above proposition with descriptive illustrations and analysis of India and other Asian countries. It will show how differing socio-psychological learning processes among the cultural elite and the majority, inhibit equal participation in the use of communication technology. Three broad areas of analysis will include : (i) gender differentiation, (ii) the language issue, and (iii) the use of communication technology, more specifically, video technology.

In order to provide an Asian perspective, a structural analysis of communication will be provided followed by the media scenario of contemporary India as a case study to understand the socio-psychological learning processes and to provide contextual framework of information overload and information underuse.

The notion of 'cultural elite' will be used throughout this report to indicate an economically, intellectually and politically powerful minority which has been ruling a large majority. In the contemporary context, it is this cultural elite group that has acquired the communication technology and skill to produce information and knowledge for their own consumption. It is why they could be designated as 'media rich' as opposed to all those who lack it but constitute the majority. They could be referred to as 'media poor'. This kind of classification is to separate those who are minority in number but dominant in control and power as opposed to those who are majority in number but who lack any control or power over the technology of communication, its prodcution, content and utilization.

The Asian Perspective

A broad cultural scenario, evolved over centuries divides most cultures between the economically and socially, rich and poor. This is true especially of Asia. Historically, while the cultural elite has had access to knowledge both oral and written; the poor have been limited only to oral information. The boundaries of these two groups are far apart, and the schism only widens leading to a serious information gap between the 'information rich' and the 'information poor'.

In the contemporary context, the sub-continent of India is a classic illustration of the differing socio-economic profiles and socio-psychological learning processes of these two groups. It is also a startling revelation of information underuse within a civilization. Indian civilization is a rich web of religious, linguistic and ecological diversities. Within 40 years of its independance, its population has doubled to about 800 million. And while there are 15 major recognised languages, over 500 dialects spoken within the country, yet some of these have so many speakers that they could constitute a large country in Europe. Multiple migrations throughout history and divergent views about life have created a complex communication mosaic. In this, apart from verbal communication, symbolic and non-verbal communication dominate, especially in inter-linguistic and pan-Indian communication. A variety of hybrid verbal languages have evolved and a whole host of universalised symbols and signs. However, there is only a small cultural elite, who are able to use this rich diversity to their advantage.

In a telephonic or day-to-day verbal conversation, or any other socially interactive situation, the use of multiple languages is fairly common in India; indeed, in the whole of South Asia. Yet again, it is an ability confined to the cultural elite. A cursory analysis of linguistic behaviour would indicate the hierarchy of language use and its connections with power—political, economic and religious. Closest to this universality is the international language 'English' which is a *lingua-franca* of the cultural elite who use the English language as an administrative and link language to communicate amongst themselves and to control power. This opens up a larger arena of communication interaction with international elites mostly in North America and Europe.

The cultural elite also use Hindi as a link language to interact with those who don't speak English but enjoy power and prestige within a linguistic region referred to as 'regional elite'. These regional elites interact and communicate with the poor in the language of the region, like Telugu, while the poor respond to them in their dialects. In this way one observes a well defined linguistic hierarchy in which the cultural elites and the regional elites act as both barriers and facilitators, in sharing knowledge and information, whether externally or internally generated. It is more so for the knowledge generated internationally through communication technologies. While the cultural elite in the social hierarchy form the apex of the obtuse cone, the information access and its percolation creates an obtuse inverted information cone in which the language barrier insulates any possibility of information percolation. In this respect, the media poor with a linguistic poverty, remain at the lowest point of the inverted information cone. Even in mono-linguistic cultures like China, this phenomenon is visible. The media poor due to their limited mobility speak only their own dialect, which serves as a means of communication within a very small geographic area. For example, a person coming from a rural area of the Indo-Gangetic plain may not be able to speak even the standard Hindi of the city. This 'poverty' of linguistic ability prevents the information poor from effectively using available information and the universalised symbols and signs.

These information discrepancies are further widened by differential access of the mass media of communication which is external in nature. The pattern of television ownership in India provides a glaring example of this. In a country of 800 million, only 7 million own TV sets, a majority of whom live in urban areas. It is these owners who also possess audio and video cassette recorders, record players, telephones, desk calculators, video games and personal computers. Their per capita annual consumer expenditure is much higher than even the average urban dweller. In this respect they present the apex of the obtuse cone. A nationwide TV audience survey with a sample of 13,304 adults (6,794 males, 6,510 females) showed that TV owners belonged to income groups several times higher than that of the average household income. They were also educated beyond high school. Their media exposure was high as they read newpapers, listened to radio, watched movies and television.

Another illustration comes from telecommunication and the pattern of telephone ownership in India. The entire telecommunication network in the Asian countries is an urban phenomenon and this being largely used by commercial companies and government machinery. In India telephone connections do not exceed three million in number. These telephones are found in the offices and homes of the cultural elite to save their time and to cut across the space barrier. It is also used as a means of controlling and spreading information among the cultural elite. On the contrary, the media poor cannot afford most of the means of receiving external information

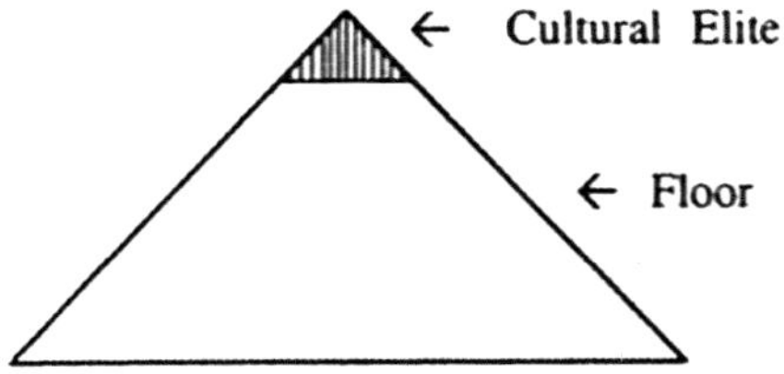

SOCIAL HIERARCHY OBTUSE CONE

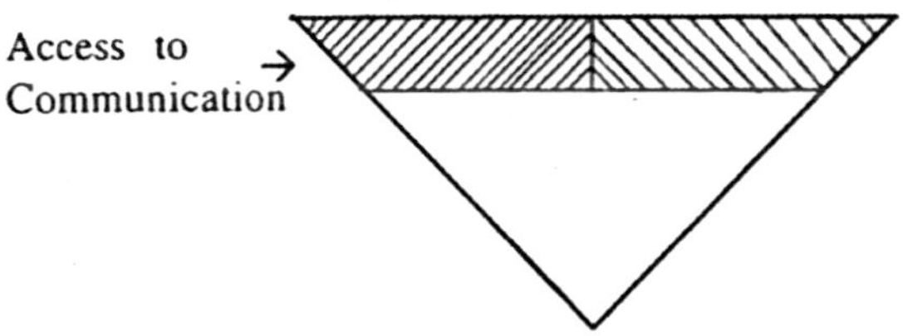

INVERTED INFORMATION CONE

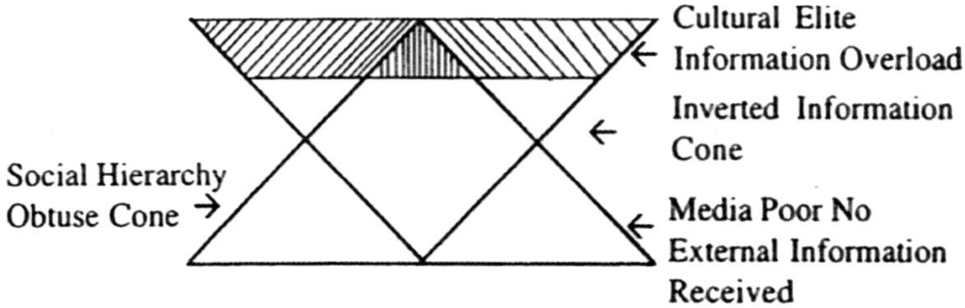

Fig 1.1 : Access to Media

through the electronic media including telecommunication. They fall below, what in India is euphemistically called the 'poverty line'. And while they struggle to get two square meals a day, they have little or no time to read; nor the ability to do so. Three-fourth of them are illiterate forming the largest part of the base of the obtuse cone.

The structural inequality of Indian civilisation goes much deeper and spreads much wider. Access to the media of communication or the lack of it are factors that impinge directly on the differing socialisation and learning processes of the media rich and poor. While learning among the media rich is both external and through socialisation, in the media poor it is exclusively through socialisation. But the durations of socialisation period that the two undergo are different.

A child coming from a media rich environment has a long duration of socialisation followed by an equally long period of adolescence in which the child acquires knowledge through external sources in a formal system of education, along with a variety of other sources, in which external agencies are involved. This includes, college and university education, both in technical and professional areas. It is during this period that learning opportunities are left wide open for the pursuit of a very broad specturm of knowledge and skill, to create new knowledge. To repetitive knowledge, new information is continuously added to broaden the horizon. In a way, the process of information over-loading continues for the media rich. While updating the knowledge, certain amount of obsolete information gets rejected, but the total process is cumulative in nature and probably this process may create a sense of information overload, the moment one begins to feel incapacitated in assimilating the information.

The media poor not only include those with no access to information but also those who still live in hunting and gathering and subsistence economies and use human and animal power for survival. In this socialisation process, the main source of acquiring knowledge, remains confined within the family and community. While describing the process of socialisation among the Yanadi a semi-nomadic tribe of India, Agrawal, Rao and Reddy (1985 : 30) observed that "There seems to be a dichotomy between the worlds of adults and children. The young children are left to play whereas adults are expected to work. It is quite common to observe the Yanadi children playing in and around the habitation throughout the day, while their parents are working somewhere in the forest...The adults are expected to provide food and shelter to the young regardless of how the children respond to the adults...A girl enters adulthood when she attains puberty. When a girl menstruates for the first time, the parents of the girl pass on the news to the girls mother's brother. He erects a small hut called *chatu gudies* near the parent's hut. In the early hours of the ninth day, the *chatu gudies* is burnt by the mother's brother and in the evening the girl is bathed in hot water and provided with new clothes...The girl is married within one or two months after attaining puberty and is declared a woman.

> "The Yanadi consider a boy an adult, when he grows a moustache and beard. Generally, when a boy starts working as a forest worker or labourer, he is treated as an adult. It is then time for him to get married. In most cases, overindulgence of the boy in sexual activities and his desire to have a wife is considered as an indication of adulthood" (1985 : 31).

The foregoing descriptive analysis is an illustration of how quickly in a tribe a child attains adulthood without passing through adolescence. To a large extent this holds true for a large number of media poor.

Given the sharp distinction between the media poor and the media rich in most of the Asian countries, it is strongly argued that it is for media rich that we can talk of information overload and information underuse. In case of the media poor, they can claim to have very little media exposure, so the question of information overload remains a hypothetical notion. If there is no externally generated information overload, the question of information underuse is not even to be considered. Therefore, the socio-cultural learning remains at the verbal level through self and participatory learning. An Indian educationist Professor J.P. Naik aptly divided the two groups into the highly inegalitarian categories of abnormal human beings: "(1) a small elite with big heads and small hands and legs which they could hardly use; and (2) a large majority of the workers who had very small heads but strong legs and hands. The system had also little scope for vertical mobility" (Naik 1980 : 128). In an Asian perspective, while discussing continuity and change in communication system, Wang and Dissanayake (1984), conceived of cultural diversity and cultural inequality as a stumbling block for any development to take place. "...Cultural imperialism and the ineffectiveness of mass media in reaching those who need change most, decision makers and planners turned their attention to the other alternatives" (Wang and Dissanayake 1984 : 26). The problems that have risen as a result of this built-in structural inequality, both in culture and communication, has antecedents and consequences for information overload and underuse in learning. In terms of consequences, one observes the emergence of several communication alliances like islands in the ocean of a given culture. Communication models evolved from the cultural experiences and studies of non-Asian countries, especially the

North American and European countries, described the communication process as linear in direction or as convergent from several uni-directional points. The latter has led to the development of the 'convergence theory'. More recently the idea of 'communication networks' have been advocated to explain the multiplicity of communication relationships (Rogers and Kincaid 1981). But all these attempts remain confined to the mono-lingual cultural settings. In the multi-lingual cultural setting, the social organisation, intermingled with linguistic diversity, generated a "super structure" of communication process which emerges in the form of "communication alliance". Like social alliance "communication alliance" is a dynamic relationship of mutual sharing, exchanging, and providing of information, knowledge and wisdom, built over a period of time. Like other social alliances, there is a continuous revision of communication alliance, thereby continuously redefining relationships among its members. The communication alliances like relationships are built horizontally, vertically and diagonally; of voluntary, involuntary and fictive kinds. Almost all vertical communication alliances are hierarchical and asymmetrical in nature, whereas horizontal and, to some extent, diagonal communication alliances are mutually symmetrical and autonomous. However, all communication alliances manifest the cultural ethos in one form or other (Agrawal 1982 : 13). These kinds of alliances divide any culture into a number of small communication alliance groups, with or without any necessarily meaningful exchange of information between any two such communication alliance groups, thereby leading to differential learning methods and acquisition of knowledge and information.

The cultural categories of media rich and media poor have helped in analysing structural factors, their antecedents and consequences in creating a hierarchy both in the learning process and knowledge and information acquisition. They have also helped to understand the notion of communication alliances and primacy of a super-structure of communication. Further, they have multiple communication boundaries fairly insulated and exclusive from each other. These communication alliances serve communication needs of each group without getting greatly influenced by the economic factors. In this respect, the economically poor are not necessarily culturally poor. Like the media rich, the media poor have their own socialisation patterns, learning processes, and means of knowledge generation and acquisition. It is only externally generated knowledge and information that is additionally available to the media rich thereby creating an unequal access to information. In order to discern the effects of externally generated information, the sources of this information must be analysed. India has been used for this case study.

The Media Scene in India

The colonial past of India has had a remarkable influence on the way the mass media evolved, got entrenched into private and public sectors and was perceived as either a means of earning money or controlling information, and thus, the thoughts of the people. It has also been shown how the colonial power perceived various forms of mass media as 'anti-establishment', 'anti-imperial' and to a large extent 'anti-ruling class'. However, to earn money they permitted the mass media, especially the print medium and cinema to grow in private sector initially controlled by their compatriots. After the First World War, the appearance of the electronic media created quite a bit of cynicism and fear in the minds of the colonial rulers who used these media as a means of control and took it into their fold as an extension of their ruling machinery. They thereby created administrative departments for the use of electronic media in most of the colonies of Britain. India was no exception. As a result in India there are two levels of control over the entire mass media. One may be referred to as a direct control; the other as indirect control.

While there is direct control on electronic media like radio, television and telecommunication, there is indirect control on the conventional media like cinema, newspapers and other print media, the latest being video, which was initially viewed as an extension of cinema. Now, even on video, both direct and indirect controls are being imposed to regulate its spread and use. It is in this broad historical perspective that one must understand, communication technology, its ownership, production, distribution and use. This will help analyse the information overload and information underuse in the Indian context, in particular, and Asia in general, and its implication for socio-cultural learning.

For the purpose of analysis mass media in India can be divided into 'government-owned' and 'private-owned' media organisations and systems as enunciated earlier. The government of India manages under its exclusive control radio, television, news documentary films and publicity, through print, cinema and the electronic media. Its documentary film production unit is one of the world's largest documentary producing organisations, responsible for a weekly Indian Newsreel dubbed in more than 15 languages. Under the terms of its liacence, every cinema house in the country is to exhibit "with each feature film an approved short film of maximum length of 609 meters". (India, 1984 : 182). Film production distribution and exhibition are privately owned, as are a large number of newspapers and advertising agencies. However, the government also spends a substantial amount on advertisements for promoting awareness about, government policies, programmes and developmental activities. The latest addition to the list of privately owned media is video, its programme production, distribution, public exhibition and manufacturing of video tape recorders and cassettes.

The Government of India ensures and regulates the quality and content of all media products by an indirect control through certification and other regulatory acts and laws. For example, the 'Registrar of Newspapers' is responsible for preparing an annual report on the country's press. This report is presented to the Indian Parliament. The Registrar has a fairly strong control as he is responsible for alloting newsprint and recommending import of printing machinery for newspaper, both being scarce commodities in India. The state through the Registrar plays an important regulatory function. Similarly no film in India can be exhibited in public before it is duly certified for exhibition by the Central Board of Film Certification. This Board plays an important role as a gate keeper. It can also stop the exhibition of films, not an uncommon experience for the film producers in India. These rules are being further extended for video exhibition in the country. Somehow, audio-cassette censorship is not known, but all the radio programmes go through a process of an in-built code of ethics for ensuring that the broadcast is in consonance with the state policy. The same holds true for television. In this way, the government-owned media are directly controlled for both production and transmission. It would be useful now, to look at each of these media separately.

Cinema

India is the world's largest film producing country. Film production and distribution engages little over 200,000 personnel. In the late seventies it had an estimated investment of about one billion US dollars (Dharap 1979: XXI). In the last five years there has been a steady growth of film production in all major languages of India. During the same period, there has been a downward trend in the production of Hindi films, which are viewed, with great enthusiasm, both in Hindi and non-Hindi speaking regions of the country. Since its inception, cinema has remained an urban phenomenon and a medium of popular entertainment, especially for the urban white and blue collar workers and to some extent the rich. Compared to the rate of over two feature films a day, the production of educational films, barring documentary films made by the government is insignificant. The same holds true for the exhibition of educational films. It would not be wrong to say that while privately funded film production gears its attention to entertainment overload, it makes very little efforts to produce programmes for learning overload. In the process, information overload remains in favour of entertainment for which no conscious effort needs to be made. And so it remains underused in the learning process, although there is social learning through demonstration.

If cinema viewing is examined, it is very clear that cinema being an urban phenomenon is viewed by a minority and that too by those who can afford to buy a ticket. Such viewers are few as there is a very high 'entertainment tax' levied by the government for the exhibition of films in theatres. The resultant effect, it seems is clearly in favour of those who can afford viewing cinema. The information load, if there is one, is of a particular genre. Film content in most cases is far removed from the socio-economic and cultural realities, to the extent of being only a fantasy. Such an information load creates cultural conflict, dissonance and alienation that cannot be converted into meaningful action, for developing the human personality. On the contrary, it favours the maintenance of a *status quo* to an extent that no new ideas can be propagated easily. To what extent this is a conscious effort needs to be carefully examined. My own hunch is that there is a very conscious effort to create celluloid images that are anti-change; favouring the reinforcement of an exploitative social structure. By doing so, it helps maintain the gap between the poor and the rich with minor aberrations keeping poor in an unreal world, trying to ape a dream world that belongs only to the rich. Due to lack of any empirical research specially socio-psychological studies, in this area, it is difficult to substantiate the proposition, with 'objective evidence'. Even then it is a 'capitalistic conspiracy' of communication as indicated by India's eminent political scientist Rajni Kothari (Kothari, April 27, 1986).

Radio

Like cinema, radio came on the Indian scene as soon as it appeared elsewhere in the world. The 60 year old medium, though started as a privately owned system of communication, was promptly taken over by the colonial government and became so important that it was declared a separate department. Among all the mass media, radio has the largest reach today in India. Almost the entire country is covered by radio signals and radio ownership is high. Some estimates indicate that it could be as high as one radio for every five households in the country. However, due to skewed distribution, majority of these sets are located in the urban areas owned by the urban rich. Therefore, fewer households of rural India have access to radio listening. In spite of these facts, radio is the only all pervasive mass media that is available to a large majority in the country. Today, more than half a million hours in about three dozen languages and an equal number of dialects are broadcast yearly in the country. The fact that All-India Radio transmits in so many languages shows that the programming pattern of radio is fairly decentralized. It follows a three-tier system of transmission—national, regional and local.

The entertainment component of radio is fairly pronounced and strong. Almost one third of this time is devoted to the commercial radio channel known as *Vividh Bharati* (Diverse India). It also devotes a fairly large percentage of its time to education and for catering to the needs of special audiences like children, women, tribal, rural and industrial workers, and personnel working in armed forces. The concept of entertainment in radio centres around songs, film music and film audio track. In this respect, the life line of entertainment of Indian radio is connected with cinema. In the Indian genre of cinema, songs are sung in almost every film, ranging from a few to a dozen per film. A majority of radio listeners and owners enjoy this kind of entertainment. This information load draws its strength largely from the existing musical tradition and repertoire of folk and classical singing forms. A deeper analysis of the content of these songs would envince that they support whole heartedly the maintenance of a *status quo*. To an extent, they act as anti-change agents and help perpetuate the acceptance of exploitative social structures. In this respect, radio entertainment remains an extension of Indian cinema in an audio form. The entire audio track of several Indian films are played on this commercial radio channel, regularly. Although the music and songs are shared equally by a large majority of both poor and rich, the audio-cassette boom has started playing a differentiating role between these two groups. There are no estimates of the pre-recorded audio-cassette sale in the country but it is very pervasive and now sold as a merchandise item on the foot-path of any commercial centre.

The information provided by radio is fairly representative in terms of news which takes up almost one-fourth of the total transmission time. Being transmitted in the mother tongue of the listener it has a large listening audience. To some extent this could pass beyond information as news of current interest. But state controlled radio suppresses certain kinds of news, and highlights certain other types. Classical music and other forms of traditional music are also presented through radio. In this respect radio and audio cassettes play a role of information multipliers but there is no information overloading, as the creation of new information is circumscribed within a state controlled radio system.

The commercial channel is considered most popular, containing a large number of commercial advertisements. These commercial advertisements interwoven with popular Indian songs, cinema audio-tracks and interviews of film personalities, have the effect of creating consumerism at national, regional and to some extent even local levels. Radio in this sense has provided support to an ever growing consumerism within the country. Coupled with this is the fact that the target audience of radio is more diversified when compared to television. Efforts are also being made to provide advertisements in local languages so as to directly reach the listeners in their own languages. This approach has widened the gulf in the aspirations of the poor and the rich. It has aroused an artificial demand and induced needs for consumer products like soft drinks and fast food, cosmetics, electronics and electrical appliances, and textiles. Studies related to radio effects are fairly obscure, but commercial advertising companies are investing quite a bit of money to measure communication effects in promoting sale of new products in the market. Some studies, however, still indicate the problem of language in radio comprehension, even though broadcasts are being made in several languages. Of course, factors like education, information level, and interest of the listeners have significant bearing upon comprehension and retention of a particular news item. The village listener generally picks up the main point of the sensational item in the news broadcast and skips most of its details and lesser news is lost on him. There could be many reasons for this. First, the villagers do not seem to comprehend fully the language or the text of the news broadcast. Secondly, they do not have the necessary background information. It seems that radio like cinema is helping to create an information gap between the information rich and information poor even though it is the most popular means of communication and has wide accessibility. (Yadava, 1983).

Television

The government-owned television—Doordarshan is one of the largest television systems in the world today. In the last five years, the growth of Indian television has been phenomenal. India was comparatively a late-comer on the international television scene, with its first television station starting only in 1959. And even that was just an experimental station.

In the last 26 years, television has grown in both scope and area. An analysis of television expansion shows that in the first decade of growth

(1959 to 1969), it remained confined to the national capital. In the second decade of expansion (1969 to 1979), the other three metropolises Bombay, Calcutta, and Madras and a few urban centres and some small rural areas were covered. The rural areas came on the television scene because of SITE—the one year Satellite Instructional Television Experiment between 1975-76.

After 1979, The IX Asian Games in 1982 occurred in the first half of the third decade of expansion. This led to the doubling of number of TV transmitters from 16 to 41, capable of receiving centralised telecast through satellite. Similarly, transmitters will multiply in the second half of the third decade of television expansion between 1984 and 1989 leading to a total of 282 transmitters as planned.

After 1985, about 70 per cent of India's population has been covered by television signals through the conventional system and hundred per cent through satellite system. But broadcasting remains centralized and most of the programmes are in two languages—Hindi and English even though there are more than 15 languages prevalent in India, as indicated earlier. In the wake of this rapid expansion, without adequate infrastructural facilities, skilled human power of organisational support, the very survival of Indian television depends on the mercy of the all pervasive commercial film industry, 'sponsored television programmes' produced by private commercial companies and some imported programmes from English speaking nations. Earlier, commercial films were used as crutches to fill television hours. Now, they have turned into a necessity, to a large extent. This has crippled the ability, capacity and creativity of the Indian television. In this respect, the creation of new information and new images remains confined in the hands of those who are accused of creating a conspiracy of communication.

Caught between conflicting but not necessarily opposing demands on the medium, Doordarshan produces and telecasts programmes for education, development and entertainment. At the same time, a large proportion of telecast time is spent in catering to the needs of the small but very vocal urban minority and to news. In this respect, if there is an information load it is for this class of television viewers. Yet studies conducted in television do not support this concept of information overload, except that parents have started talking about information diversion from education to television. Television, being an alternate means of cinema viewing, has helped increase access to cinema to the tune of almost 50 million viewers every weekend. This has meant larger access to selected television owners, but has it increased access to new information, acting either as an agent or catalyst of social change? The answer is negative, and therefore, it must be argued that television expansion in India has in no way increased the information overload. Instead it has provided an alternate means to the same information earlier available through cinema or other entertainment industries. To a large extent the same could be said about information related to news and current affairs. In television, news is borrowed directly from the news copy of All-India Radio with a few insertions of visuals. At this stage television development in India could only be characterised as an 'information multiplier' rather than 'information generator'. And the learning, if any is impaired by limited access to the medium, which is less than one per cent of the total population.

The Print Medium

In a largely illiterate country like India, where two-thirds of the population cannot read and write, the print medium has an insignificant role to play for information dissemination and learning. However, in quantitative terms, the reach of the print medium is staggering. In 1984 "newspapers were brought out in 85 languages. Apart from the sixteen principal languages, newspapers were published in 69 other languages, and a few foreign languages. The highest number of newspapers were published in Hindi (5,655) followed by English (3,689)" (India, 1984 : 170). The circulation figure crossed the 5 million mark in 1982. However, when these figures are compared with the total population the ratio is phenomenally low.

As indicated earlier, the majority of newspapers and periodicals are privately owned in contrast to the electronic media. The news agencies are also privately owned, important among these being the Press Trust of India (PTI), United News of India (UNI), Samachar Bharati and Hindustan Samachar. In addition the government has the Press Information Bureau to act as a channel of communication between the government and the mass media. The Press Information Bureau is responsible for providing information about government policies, programmes and activities to various news agencies, media organisations both within the country and abroad. It also provides news and photographs to the press through distribution of press material. On the whole, there is an invisible control over the print medium especially the press, and therefore, also a fine filter process involved in news generation and publication. The private ownership having a profit motive as a main criterion for running the press, gives its own twists and turns to news and information in India. Recently, some eminent media persons observed that there is very little difference that one can find between the headlines carried by the privately owned press and government owned radio and television. In both the cases, the reasons for this commonality may be different. But it becomes equally important to point out that there is a great deal of uniformity in Indian media. This is because it is meant to cater to a class of cultural elite, whose learning behaviour and information needs are quite different from a large majority who are far away from any print medium. The printed word is a key to success, for the minority, a means to control power, a method to manipulate people and a strategy to reap the fruits in a small group without distributing these to a large majority.

The question of information overload even for the minority in the print medium is far from the reality as within the so called literate minority only a microscopic section is able lay its hand on the vast store of information within and outside India. This microscopic population is basically English speaking, internationally connected, and a highly motivated group, linked in a network leading a non-Indian life. If this small group has an information overload it is because of its own desire to keep up with the rest of the world, to continuously strive for competition with international elite and to emulate their counter-part in the rest of the world. The question of overload of information in the print medium for the large majority of Indians does not arise and the question of underuse, an absurdity.

Gender Factor in Information Underuse

It is now common knowledge that in South Asian Countries, the learning opportunities are unequal with regard to male and female children. It is typically the female child who is left out from the formal educational system and if there is a choice between the two, encouragement is given to the male child. This differential treatment is inherent in the very social structure where men dominate over women, enjoying such a degree of freedom and privilege that a double standard of morality is the expected norm for them. In a very broad sense men and women live in two separate worlds and the realisation of these worlds comes even before the child is born. After birth, this realisation becomes accute and the separation of the two worlds is complete, much before a girl attains puberty. Agrawal and Rai (1980) have aptly described, this separation while conducting a rural study in western India, with special reference to rural women in the state of Rajasthan.

> "Differentiation (between the male and female child) begins just after the birth of the baby. If a boy is born, the midwife is paid twice the rate generally given for a girl if born...The midwife is given a new *chunari* (a piece of long cloth for covering the head), one kg., of jaggery and five kgs. of mixed grains. A drum or a brass plate is beaten to announce the birth of a male child. The village women are invited to sing songs and sweets are distributed especially on the birth of first son. The husband's younger brother is called to bury the umbilical cord. In high and intermediate jatis, husband's sisters get gifts like gold or silver ornaments according to the condition of the household whereas among scheduled castes, clothes are given as gifts. These are some of the ways of expressing happiness on the birth of a son. But no such fanfare or celebration is done in case daughter is born" (Agrawal and Rai, 1980 : 54).

In rural Rajasthan very few girls are sent to school. Instead they move around with the group in the village. Disciplining of daughters is left entirely to the mothers, who also try and teach them household work. The daughters are first taught to sweep the house and cattle shed in the morning. For this mothers wake up their daughters early in the morning and let the sons sleep for some more time.

In the school going age, when sons go to school, daughters stay at home even if they are interested in going to school. Daughters are not sent to school, as the parents think that it is a waste of time. During this time they can do household work and help the mother or look after the young children. Instead of sending daughters to school they prefer to send them to field or for cattle grazing. The girls go to school only if they have a strong desire to study. The older girls who study till fourth and fifth classes are allowed to go to school, only, if they have finished some of the household work. (Agrawal and Rai 1980 : 59-60).

The foregoing descriptive analysis though very region specific and culture specific is fairly representative of how gender differentiation takes place in the Asian context, especially in South Asia. It has a remarkable influence on communication behaviour, and consequently on information use. A detailed analysis of cultural communication indicates that it is highly verbal "...involving in most of the cases, interpersonal communication between women and very little between male and female (Agrawal and Rai 1980 : 65). At the household level which is a smallest unit for any meaningful and continuous communication, it is generally either hierarchical or vertical where instructions flow from top to bottom and from men to women. Even in personal matters, a woman is expected to seek approval from the males of the household be it the father, husband, father-in-law, or brother. Basically communication is sharply divided between the men's and women's worlds. "The communication and interaction between parents and children and husband and wife, that too in privacy, is the only way these two halves are linked in the women's world". (Agrawal and Rai 1980 : 75).

At the community level, the 'external information' is generally obtained, by women through men and very little through mass media. It is also because there is very little information that could be commonly needed by all the women of the village. In terms of mass media access, it was observed that women in general had almost zero access; first due to in built structural inequality and secondly due to limited need for information.

Table 1.1 provides a glimpse of media possession in rural India including the village of Rajasthan discussed here. It is evident from the Table 1.1 that the average media ownership is very low. It is important to note that these media are owned by men, with the women having little or no access even though the media are available within household.

Table 1.2 shows that even when television was available equally to men and women of seven villages, it was more men than women who viewed television in a community viewing situation.

Given a social situation where information saturation is relatively high for men as calculated in terms of availability, the long duration of transmission will not change the underuse by women. This is much more so in South Asia, where there are built-in methods of negating any possibility of information use by women thereby leading to high-level of information underuse. For example, cinema viewing in most cases is a male pre-occupation. Even when a storyline of a film is woman oriented, dealing with women's issues and problems, it will be largely viewed by men. Even a casual observation of cinema viewing behaviour in India would indicate that more than two-thirds of the seats would be occupied by males, at any time. Even in the household situation, while viewing television or listening to the radio, the men are not supposed to be disturbed, whereas a woman could accept interruption at any time for any reason. Similar illustrations of a variety of situations can be given of how gender is a factor of information underuse.

Table 1.1 : Percentage Distribution of Households Processing Radio or Transistor Subscribing Newspaper and having Cinema going During SITE

Sr. No.	*Village name*	*Total households*	*% of radio owning households*	*% of newspaper subscribing households*	*% of Cinema going member's households*
1.	Kawadpalley	221	15.8	2.3	73.3
2.	Ismailpur	172	5.2	0.0	11.0
3.	Pothnal	246	8.9	1.6	30.1
4.	Sakarra	240	12.9	10.0	13.8
5.	Ghenupali	173	3.5	5.8	10.4
6.	Khedli	165	3.2	0.0	17.3
7.	Dadusar	276	12.7	4.7	31.5
	Average	212	9.9	3.8	28.3

Source : Agrawal (1978 : 40)

Table 1.2 : Percentage Distribution of Television Viewers by Sex During SITE

Sr. No.	*Name of Village*	*Male Viewer*	*Female Viewer*	*Total Numbers of Viewers*
1.	Kawadpalley	62.5	37.5	381
2.	Ismailpur	72.5	27.5	171
3.	Pothnal	81.8	18.2	220
4.	Sakarra	55.8	44.2	912
5.	Ghenupali	56.7	43.3	420
6.	Khedli	63.0	37.0	511
7.	Dadusar	61.7	38.3	543
	Average	61.6	38.4	451.2

Source : Agrawal (1970 : 54)

An analysis of programme content, especially of film and television, reveals very startling but well-known facts about gender factors in information overload and information underuse. Though there are very few content analysis studies available on which to base any definitive conclusions, it is common knowledge and very apparent to a viewer with sensitive eyes and ears that film and television in India, with rare exceptions, perpetuates a traditional role for women. Any deviation, in the end, is contrived to make the woman conform to the image of the idealised Indian woman as a good wife, mother and sister. "To the weight of this tradition is added a Victorian hypocrisy which still dominates the thinking of westernised Indians—a middle class [cultural elite] morality which makes a sharp distinction between woman as wife and mother, and woman as mistress and lover" (Vasudev 1983 : 37). Further, Vasudev observes in the Indian film that "the pinnacle of ambition for a woman is marriage, of achievement, the birth of a son. Within marriage, her role is clearly delineated. If, for whatever reason, she deviates from it, it is seen as a betrayal of her biological and functional role and she must pay a price in humiliation and defeat" (Vasudev 1983 : 38). This, in many ways, reflects the predominantly orthodox and traditional view about women on the Indian film. In the ultimate analysis, "women are seldom shown as understanding or supportive of each other. They are, in fact, the preservers of tradition and each others' worst persecutors, while male camaraderie has always been strong and emphasized in most films" (Vasudev 1983 : 42).

Television, in its rapid expansion and its heavy dependence on Indian film helps to reinforce what was already portrayed in Indian films. Chandiram and Agrawal (1982 : 163) observed that on Indian television "generally, women characters continue to be portrayed in their inferior position compared to man in an asymmetrical relationship in which domestic chores and 'mother' image are predominant. There are very few plays, which depict women trying to cope with the stress of urban living and the moral and physical strength to sustain man's aggression. These characterizations hold true for newly married women, but to some extent, the older women in certain situations are portrayed as strong, dominant and authoritative figures, able to cope with any calamity that may befall the family".

In the recent past, the floodgate of serials and slick advertisements on Indian television has been opened, leading to further degeneration of the woman as an object to sell products and as a show-piece and always in a supportive role to man. While this has been the case with urban women of the cultural elite, the rural women, especially the media poor, are completely left out or are portrayed as beautiful, innocent village belles, ready to be lured by smart young men. Looking from this perspective, two factors emerge very clearly : one, mass media is *pro-status quo vis-a-vis* women, two, it is anti-change *vis-a-vis* women. The related point is that media exposure is high for the cultural elite women, whereas media poor women are even worse of than their menfolk in terms of media access. In this respect, while there is a media overload for the media rich women, there is a complete dearth of media exposure for media poor women. Accepting that there is influence of media on behaviour, it is evident that the information overload is helping the women in India to learn to live in the traditional confines. Gender as a factor in information overload while perpetuating the *status quo* for media rich women, leaves a large majority without any tangible effects. Hence, there is no question of information underuse.

Language and the Question of Information Overload and Underuse

At the outset, it is important to indicate that in a large part of Asia, multi-lingualism is a way of life. India provides a classic example of this life. An average Indian lives in multiple linguistic worlds'. A language to communicate with parents and family members, another to deal with the employer and peer outside home. A third language to deal with bureaucracy, Government and the State. A fourth language for being a part of the national and international literary class and to acquire knowledge. A casual observation in India is that social interaction even among persons belonging to the same linguistic region, bewilders, non-Asian scholars, because of the way multiple languages are used. A sentence in normal conversation quite often contains two to three languages and the method of sentence construction would appear quite bizarre for a mono-lingual speaker. Such a siuation is not only acceptable for good communication but considered normal. In this kind of multilinguistic communication context, if one analyses the communication ability, while the media rich may excel in the use of multiple languages having an equally good command of several language and skilfull mixing of multiple languages for communication, the media poor remain confined within a narrow bound of communication ability, with limited vocabulary, that too in a particular dialect of a language. This generates an inherent inequality both in terms of communication ability and social interaction. At the same time it creates a natural barrier for receiving externally generated information and knowledge, beyond the boundaries of a given language.

In 1973, while working on Satellite Instructional Television Experiment (SITE), I confronted the twin problem of language and television in the Indian context. After ten years once again, while working as a member of the 'working group' on 'Software Plan for Doordarshan', this issue assumed an even larger dimension in the national perspective. In years to come, with the enormous expansion of Indian mass media the issue is going to become emotionally tense and will assume greater relevance for the topic under discussion. It is going to raise some very serious soul searching questions, for language and communication in the multilingual, multi-religious and multi-ethnic civilization of India. A historical perspective is intended here, to indicate how important the issue is, both at the intellectual and national levels while discussing information overload and information underuse.

Satellite in India have provided the enormous power of reaching every part of the country through a satellite signal. The technology was historically designed for reaching viewers, who have had a common language to speak with marginal variations in their speech behaviour and who have in many ways, learnt to share common verbal and non-verbal symbols, images and identities. In a situation like this, satellite communication provides an enormous multiplying ability at the least cost without hurting anyone's sensitivities, symbolic and cognitive domains. On the contrary, in a multi-linguistic and multi-religious country like India, it has compounded enormous difficulties both for viewers and communicators. At the same time it has provided unlimited reach for a centralized transmission capacity in which a single image with a single language is thrust upon all viewers disregarding their cultural, linguistic, and social diversities.

Given the historical background of India, it is known that there are very few common religio-economic and social occasions with the same historical and symbolic manifestations that could be projected on the television screen to provide a common experience. Each communication alliance group has something to share and some information to exchange. However, these alliances do not necessarily share anything in common at the national level. Nor are there any common processes in the learning experience, that would enable them to share and exchange meaningful and comprehensible information. The net effect is, that although there is a common information pool available, structural constraints prevent the sharing of information and knowledge. And the mono-linguistic television grammar does not permit any common sharing of experiences across the nation. The situation is compounded by socially stratified communication alliances in each linguistic region. It is precisely for this reason that television is now only viewed by the media rich instead of being used "as an aid for achieving cultural independance and building our national cultural identity" (An Indian Personality for Television, 1985 : 28). It has now turned into a cultural appendage for the national elite. In this process, language as a vital means of communication, apart from visual images, has further divided the media rich from the media poor at two levels—first at economic and secondly at the linguistic level. It has also led to the search for those television programmes which rely upon crude non-verbal symbols and development of 'hybird language' or a 'popular linguistic code'. These are divorced from the day-to-day communicative language, used in any given linguistic region of India by the media poor. This is especially true to Hindi cinema, which is telecast regularly on Indian television for the entire country. Once again, except for political outbursts in some of the linguistic regions, it is assumed that the audience in general, like to view Hindi movies on Indian television. My hunch is, that an average television viewer would prefer to see culturally decodable images and linguistically comprehensible words. It is only when this requirement is fulfilled that a viewer would look for variety and images from other cultures and languages, including non-Indian images. Therefore, until multiple languages are used in television, the seemingly information overload, through satellite communication, is highly underused by a minority.

All-India Radio (AIR) a government-owned radio broadcasting system has over half a century evolved methods of communication in the language of a given region, thereby recognising that without language no verbal communication will be possible. All-India Radio continues to broadcast radio programmes for different dialect groups within a given language area. These are continuously evaluated and introduced as and when required. The field publicity organisation of the Ministry of Information and Broadcasting, Government of India, has reported time and again that the documentaries produced by the Films Division of India (another government owned unit for documentary production) are not comprehended by a large majority of rural viewers due to variation in dialects of the given region. Similar experiences have been expressed by civil servants and others who visit the interior parts of the country in any linguistic region. The question one would like to raise is whether it would be appropriate to talk of information overload or underuse without first raising the question of language, if communication has to be effective. In the context of India and in many other Asian countries this issue has assumed political overtones and in many ways has acted as an inhibitor of learning from radio and other forms of mass media.

Lessons from Rural Television in India and Indonesia

During the Satellite Instructional Television Experiment (SITE), in India ten village studies using anthropological methods and techniques were conducted in seven States. These studies were conducted by anthropologists who lived in medium sized villages having a multi-*jati* (multi-caste) population and located away from the urban centre. One of the ten villages selected for this purpose was a predominantly tribal village in Orissa, a state of India. The second Study focussed specially on the women of a village in Rajasthan, another State of India. The remaining eight villages were selected from among seven states of the country namely Andhra Pradesh, Bihar, Karnataka, Orissa, Rajasthan and Gujarat. For this study anthropologists lived in selected villages for intensive data collection to understand the process of human communication and effects of satellite television on the rural structure. Communication was considered as "the process of transmitting information from a source to a receiver, with the intention of affecting behaviour change" (Agrawal 1978 : 5). The source in this case was satellite communication and the behaviour that was to be modified was that of rural television viewers. After 18 months of intensive field work, some of the most important conclusions drawn were that, "the comparison of the language spoken in the village and the TV programme language suggests possible loss of message-comprehension, specially in the Hindi speaking clusters. Serious efforts are required to develop a new common language to be used in TV programme-production for large areas like Bihar, Madhya Pradesh and Rajasthan and for future national satellite-based television". (Agrawal 1978 : 79).

A similar conclusion was drawn for the states of Andhra Pradesh, Gujarat, Karnataka and Orissa, but to a lesser degree. The most revealing conclusions were drawn from the state of Gujarat. Anthropologists observed that due to use of *Chaurouturi* (a dialect of Gujarati), comprehension of the programmes was very high even through it created quite a bit of displeasure amongst the Gujarati literary class. The linguistic profile of the villages under study, indicated that the languages spoken in the villages and those used in the television programme production differ quite a bit as there was a tendency to use standard language, which the viewers were not familiar with. At the same time, when the programmes were produced in a studio located within the viewers' linguistic area, language was not usually a barrier in comprehending the programme". Shukla and Kumar (1977) observed that language development as a result of television viewing was higher among school children in those linguistic regions where production facilities were located within the linguistic area. These observations are significant while discussing the issue of language and information overload and underuse.

Women and Television

While conducting SITE study on Rajasthan it was observed that, "cultural communication in Khedli (village) is exclusively verbal, area and situation specific, involving in most of the cases, interpersonal communication between women and very little between male and female". (Agrawal and Rai, 1980 : 65). This may hold true about women in large parts of rural India. The need to communicate in languages other than those spoken in the village is extremely limited and also not considered essential. The anthropologist working in Khedli observed that she had to learn a great deal of local language in order to communicate with these women, an experience fairly common to any rural research. The same holds true for television viewing. For example, during SITE, the use of standard Hindi created a high level of discontent among the women TV viewers, leading to lack of comprehension, even though these programmes were telecast in a so-called Hindi-speaking region of Rajasthan. The question raised here is, that it is not enough to talk about a language like Hindi in programme production for a large region. The important thing is to map our meaningful linguistic regions for the purpose of television production, to make it comprehensible for the viewer, especially the women who have limited access to mass media and linguistic ability to communicate beyond the dialect of a language. The analysis only reaffirms that learning through television or for that matter mass media is possible in the language of the region. Therefore, the use of any standard language may on the surface give the feeling of providing information and the repetitive transmission gives the feeling of information overload. But it certainly does not mean information overload. And then the question of its underuse does not arise. As a matter of fact it is more information non-use.

Television and the Indian Child

The socialization process includes learning of language and related cultural symbols and meanings. Beyond family, kin-group and educational institutions, television, like other mass-media has started playing an important role of an agent for socialization. Even though a very small minority of Indian children have an access to television, like adults they do view television programmes. An analysis of children's television programmes has indicated that the majority of television programmes for young children or pre-school children are in the English language. How far these English programme create cultural confusion in the minds of young children is not known. However, it would not be wrong to say that the children get glued to television and probably constitute the largest single majority of avid television viewers. Can television help multi-lingual learning, almost an essential aspect of living in a multi-linguistic country? Or will it create a built in inferiority for the 'mother tongue'? At present, very little effort has been made, both for the children of media rich and media poor. However, while children of the media rich may be able to take advantage of advances in communication, for the children of media poor it would constitute information non-use.

In Indonesia, exactly after 17 days of the completion of SITE, in India, on August 17, 1976, a satellite-based television system was introduced with the help of the Indonesian domestic communications satellite, known as *Palapa* I. This opened up the possibility of using satellite for public education and information especially for those who lived in rural Indonesia and in the far flung 13,677 islands constituting the largest archipelago in the world. The initial research evaluation, jointly conducted by the Communication Institute of the East-West Centre, United States of America and the Indonesian National Institute of Economic & Social Research (LEKNAS/LIPI), provided interesting comparative data showing how language can act as a barrier even though *Bahasa* Indonesia is generally spoken by a large majority in Indonesia. The original study was conducted "to assess the impact of satellite transmitted television on rural development in Indonesia by using a longitudinal research design". (Alfian, Abdullah and Chu : 1979 : 5). One of the studies conducted for the evaluation had followed anthropological methods and techniques for data collection by Budhisantoso (1979). It is interesting to note that the finding of Budhisantoso in Indonesia reaffirm what was observed in India earlier, on the language issue.

"Modern plays, popularly known as *sandiwara*, have audiences representing all age categories. As entertainment, *sandiwara* occupies a significant position in the television schedule, especially for the less educated villagers, who prefer simple shows. In fact, most of the dramas shown on television take no longer than 40 minutes and are generally screened between 8.50 p.m. and 9.40 p.m., just before bedtime. Unlike many films shown on television, the dialogue of *sandiwara* is in simple Bahasa Indonesia and focuses on family life, a familiar theme for most village audiences which accounts for the popularly of these programmes:

> "The programmes listed as favourites demonstrate how the villagers accept what they consider to be congruent with their interest. News, popular music, religious forms and light entertainment are compatible with the interests of most villagers..."

"None of them name "English Lesson" as a favourite programme, simply because they do not really feel the need. Unlike teachers or educated people who seek cultural enrichment by communicating with the English speaking world, none of the villagers were interested in the English programme..."

"Nor was there much interest in the Bahasa Indonesia instruction. Most villagers did not feel the necessity to improve their Bahasa Indonesia, but were interested in information on where and how to buy cheaper kerosene and clothes..."

"An example of this was found in Aceh where an old man was sitting in front of a television set, alone, except for a field worker there to observe television viewing habits. The man appeared to be following a programme on good and correct (*baik dan benar*) Bahasa Indonesia. The field-worker was surprised at the man's interest in the programme, but was even more surprised when, at the conclusion of the programme, the man asked what had been discussed. Apparently, he had been unable to follow the instructor, who had been speaking in grammatically correct Bahasa Indonesia. In fact, the language instruction given on the television programme is often quite difficult for even high school seniors to follow. Most of the programme is devoted to showing the difference between correct grammer and vocabulary, and the common mistakes made in daily conversation. Reactions similar to the old man's were found in West Java, West Kalimantan, and Bali after the villagers had viewed educational programmes, which were generally presented in Bahasa Indonesia without pictorial aids." (Budhisantoso 1979 : 315-318).

Several such examples could be cited to support the view that language, both as a facilitator and inhibitor can play a critical role in information underuse or non-use, which is what has been demonstrated in the two examples of India and Indonesia. Its critical role in socio-cultural learning must also not be undermined. Communication alliances of the media poor and the media rich further complicates the matter, thereby reducing the information use to a substantial level in Asia. It is therefore, argued that the concept of information overload must be reformulated in the light of these observations and information under-use should be re-examined in the light of marginal or non-use of information within the existing cultural milieu of linguistic multiplicity.

Video

The latest craze on the Indian media scene is the 'video', which has penetrated the remotest part of the country. Any analysis of video penetration indicates that it has been exclusively used for film viewing. After 1982, India saw an unprecedented boom of video viewing several times more than cinema and television viewing. Video emerged on the Indian scene as soon as it appeared in Europe and America. Within less than six years since its arrival its penetration in the remotest rural hamlets and inaccessible terrains of India is something incomprehensible to a large majority of social scientists and communication researchers. Cinema, another visual medium having a history of more than eight decades remains an urban phenomena, whereas video in less than six years has surpassed all the viewing records of cinema in India. And India is one of the largest film producing countries of the world. One would be interested in raising some issues *vis-a-vis* the information overload emerging as a result of this all pervasive penetration in the Indian cultural milieu. Also it would be appropriate to raise the question of socio-cultural learning that takes place or will take place through video as an information multiplier, a toy of the rich and a means to decentralize information access.

Video is being used for advertising by inserting advertisements in films on video, which has helped reduce the cost of pre-recorded cassettes. Another use is in the areas of training of personnel and other informal groups like Self-Employed Women's Association (SEWA), a trade union for education and training of a group of largely illiterate women. Video is also being used for political purposes. Now, it is increasingly being used for keeping a record of special occasions like marriages and birthdays. I have recently tried to analyse the socio-cultural implications of video penetration in India. In terms of the socio-cultural effects of video, it is expected that it will widen the information gap instead of bridging it, which was the original aim of all government owned communication media meant for the masses in India. While the penetration of information has been beyond the wildest hopes, video will, and to some extent, already has created new 'social groups' in the form of 'video viewers' and 'non-video viewers' or 'TV viewers'. Privatisation of entertainment, inherent in the class system in the feudal era, is again becoming an aspect of modern day. Today an average Indian makes a clear distinction between video television and cinema, both in terms of technology and genre of programme contents.

It evokes multiple and contrasting reactions. Among the urban educated with connections abroad, video has assumed an important reference point to initiate discussions whether in a drawing room or at a market-place or even while travelling. It has assumed a special meaning for the youth of this class who have started using the class-room for exchanging video tapes instead of class-notes. It has created a new arena of social competition, social prestige and a new kind of media consumption. On another plane any reference to video, especially among the adults and socially conscious parents, creates a sense of loss and gloom as they begin to express the undesirable effects video has on the studies of their children in all age groups and effects on the cultural ethos and morality. Some even complain about bad effects on health due to video viewing. Within six years, video has passed the stage of craze and has been accepted as an 'essential' item by an elite group as a means of recreation and entertainment. "Its operation, continuous supply of pre-recorded video cassettes, and above all the uninterrupted import of video cassette recorders has taken the Indian men and women, whether urban or rural, by storm. It has become a phenomenon without any parallel". (Agrawal 1985 : 1).

Video, as a technology, has provided flexible and instantaneous means of information production and distribution in the Indian context. Yet once again it is being largely used as an information distributor and multiplier, but not as an information creator. It has been used in a very small way for the mobilization of masses to act as a change agent. In this respect, it has not contributed much to the learning process and hence question of overload does not arise. Also it has not substituted in any substantial way the cultural learning process.

In other words video remains within the realm of maintaining the existing structure and providing information overload if any to the cultural elite.

The foregoing analysis presented leaves very little doubt in my mind that without examining the social structure, either at a micro or macro level, it will be a partial analysis of information overload and underuse in the learning process. The socio-cultural perspective of learning in the Indian milieu and in Asia does not differ strikingly. In both cases the structural predicaments in the contemporary context will remain the most important stumbling blocks in providing equal opportunities of learning. And in this way, while the cultural elite will be overloaded with information and knowledge, the poor will have very little or nothing to gain.

REFERENCES

Agrawal, Binod C. (1978). *Television comes to Village : An Evaluation of SITE.* Ahmedabad : Space Applications Centre.

Agrawal, Binod C. (1982). Communication Structures in India : A Case Study of Television. *Communicator*, Vol. XVII (4) : pp. 12-15.

Agrawal, Binod C. (1985). Video Flow in India. UNESCO/BRU Project. Ahmedabad : Development and Educational Communication Unit.

Agrawal, Binod C. (1985). Video—a new diversion for India's rich. *Media Development*, Vol. XXXII (1) : pp. 14-15.

Agrawal, Binod C. and Kumkum Rai (1980). *Women, Television, and Rural Development: An Evaluative Study of SITE in a Rajasthan Village.* Ahmedabad : Space Applications Centre.

Agrawal, Rao, and Reddy (1985). *Yanadi Response to Change : An Attempt in Action Anthropology.* New Delhi : Concept Publishing Company.

Alfian, T. Abdullah and Godwin Chu (1979). Introduction. In *Satellite Television in Indonesia.* Alfian and Godwin Chu. Honolulu (eds) : East-West Communication Institute.

Budhisantoso, S. (1979). Initial Reaction to Television in Indonesian Village. In *Satellite Television in Indonesia.* eds. Alfian and Godwin Chu. Honolulu : East-West Communication Institute, pp. 291-324.

Chandiram, Jai and Binod C. Agrawal (1982). Towards Equality : Women in Indian Television. *Media Asia*, Vol. 9(3) : pp. 161-65.

Dharap, B.V. (1979). *Indian Films 1977 and 1978.* Pune : Motion Picture Enterprise.

Kothari, Rajni (1986). Flight into the 21st Century. *Times of India*, April 27, 1986.

Naik, J.P. (1980). Educational and Vocational Preparation of Children. In *Profile of the Child in India. Politics and Programmes*, New Delhi : Ministry of Social Welfare, Government of India, pp. 127-144.

Rogers, Everett, M. and D.L. Kincaid (1981). *Communication Networks.* New York : The Free Press.

Shukla, Snehlata and Kuldip Kumar (1977). *SITE Impact Study on Children.* Bangalore: : Indian Space Research Organisation.

Vasudev, Aruna (1983). The Woman : Vamp or Victim. In *Women and Media : Analysis Alternatives and Action.* Kamla Bhasin and Bina Agrawal (eds). New Delhi : Kali, pp. 37-43.

Wang, Georgette and Wimal, Dissanayake (1984). Indigenous Communication System and Development : A Reappraisal. In *Continuity and Change in Communication Systems : An Asian Perspective.* Georgette Wang and Wimal Dissanayake (eds). Norwood : Ablex Publishing Corporation, pp. 21-36.

Yadava, J.S. (1983). *Multi-Level Information System for Integrated Rural Development Programme in India.* New Delhi : Indian Institute of Mass Communication.

Reports

India 1984 : A Reference Annual New Delhi : Ministry of Information and Broadcasting, Government of India.

India 1985 : A Reference Annual New Delhi : Ministry of Information and Broadcasting, Government of India.

Mass Media in India (1983) Mass Media in India. New Delhi : Ministry of Information and Broadcasting, Government of India.

Anonymous (1985) An Indian Personality for Television. Vol. 1. Report of the working group on Software for Doordarshan. New Delhi : Ministry of Information and Broadcasting, Government of India.

2

CULTURE AND COMMUNICATION TECHNOLOGY IN THE INDIAN HIGHER EDUCATION

A Synergy or a Mismatch

BINOD C. AGRAWAL

A DEBATE in which a large number of educationists and technologists are deeply involved pertains to major breakthroughs in chip technology having an all-pervasive influence at the global level. One of the aspects that is of concern to teachers of higher education is its multiple applications and uses for improving the quality of higher education and its spread. Recently, a large number of technologists have objected to the term 'new' when talking of communication technologies. In their opinion, the technologies are not new; what has gone through remarkable transformations is its applications, resulting from the initiatives taken by the transnationals to convert the chip technology into consumer electronics for mass consumption.

There is quite a bit of discussion on 'Communication Revolution' in both national and international arena. The basic assumption in these discussions centres around two points. One, that communication technologies are equally available, accessible and useful to the whole population of a country like India. Two, the user of these technologies would more or less respond to the communication technology uniformly. It is in this area that the applications of the communication technologies have assumed new meaning and relevance for higher education. Also, the cost of classroom education has increased and enhancement of the quality of such education requires technological intervention beyond chalk and blackboard, for discussing, explaining and describing the latest scientific findings.

Aim

The broad perspective in which there is a felt need for the use and intervention of technologies, especially of communication technologies, for higher education will be discussed in this paper. In order to examine the context of the use of technologies in higher education, the cultural milieu will be described in the historical and social perspectives. To what extent the technologies would be an aid in promoting the quality and spread of higher education will be analysed and the degree to which the choice and mode of usage of these technologies will be crucial, will be highlighted.

The Indian Society and Culture : A Continuity of 5000 Years

There are several layers of reality that emerge when we talk of Indian society and culture. India has a cultural reality that has evolved over several millennia while its political boundaries are waxing and waning. This cultural reality provided a mosaic that resulted in a composite picture at a macroscopic level, depicting it to be an unified whole. But on another level, the linguistic and independent evolution of several cultural tradition emerge equally to provide another level of cultural reality that seemed equally distinct and autonomous. Over a period of time, it became increasingly difficult to call each of these traditions a part of the larger whole which is what India is today as a political reality. In this perspective, it would be erroneous to call India a whole today.

At another level, the Indian society from the very beginning of its history remained extremely stratified and heirarchical in nature. This characterization of Indian society in its contemporary form has assumed an enormous complexity as a result of industrialization, westernization and continually increasing urbanization. Democratic processes, which are supposed to reduce such fission tendencies were on many occasions found to be strengthening the ever-increasing both horizontal and vertical cleavages within the overarching cultural and political boundaries.

However, the religious ethos which has provided a powerful unifying force within this framework has dwindled due to invasions or other religious beliefs. The net outcome is what the contemporary India looks like, having a large unidentified, incomprehensible, seemingly static and unknown mass of humanity, ruled and governed by a very small elite, continuously going through metamorphoses to adapt to the changing world scene. History bears testimony to several rulers and invaders who came to India and went without seriously scratching the broad social fabric of Indian society and culture.

Education, per se, whether in the classical sense or in the contemporary context was and remains a victim of the very structure in which it flourished. From the ancient days and even today it remains a preserve of the few. It would not be wrong to say that the Indian society is divided between the rulers having 'power' of education and the ruled without education. This bipartite division of Indian society seemed to have been tempered for the first time by the British education that allowed seemingly an open admission policy for brilliant students without any discrimination, a legacy that we continue to follow without any appreciable effect on the cultural ethos or psyche of the Indian society.

Out of over 800 million people there is a small number, less than 2 to 5 per cent of visible rich and a maddeningly large number (95 to 98%) of the poor. The visible rich, mostly living in urban areas have television sets at home and are in the process of acquiring many more latest communication technologies. A large number of them (both men and women) have the benefit of getting higher education including professional education within India and abroad. It is this class which can be characterized as being influenced by the 'Communication Revolution' and getting drawn into the growing international information society. If the term communication revolution is used for them, it would not be wrong to say that the future education system, at all levels, including higher education would be under great pressure to accept the new communication technologies to gain information and knowledge.

On the contrary, half of the India's population below poverty line (see Dholakia, 1978, and Ojha, 1971) do not earn enough to get two meals a day. For them formal education of any kind is a luxury and they belong to the world's largest uneducated humanity of any country. Leaving exceptions, none in this class has had occasion to benefit from higher education except being exploited and repressed by the educated. The other 40 per cent who are above poverty line, but falling in the category of the poor, barely manage to scrape through and whose children, also a large majority, have not seen the doors of higher learning.

Serious efforts on the part of the Government of India to elevate the scheduled caste and scheduled tribes into the mainstream through higher education has helped a small minority to reap the fruits of education. Another group women also falls within the deprived sections who have been largely out of the higher education system. The net result is that (parenthesis) the total students enrolled in 1983-84 were 3.5 million spread over 124 universities and 15 institutions deemed universities and 5246 colleges—less than 0.5 per cent of India's population where more than 40 per cent persons are in the youth category. This analysis further supports the view that higher education remains a luxury for a large fraction of India's population and so when we are talking of communication technologies for higher education : are we going to use communication technologies to improve the quality of education for the rich? or will we use new communication technologies to spread higher education to large masses? We tend to take the view that the communication technologies ought to be responding to the needs of the spread of education while assisting to improve the quality of education.

Cultural Ethos and Higher Education

It would be important at this juncture to discuss the meaning of cultural ethos *vis-a-vis* higher education. The contemporary cultural ethos is such that even after having glaring inequality between the minority educated and majority uneducated, it has only led to the exploitation of the silent majority without any open confrontation or retaliation from the majority. Historically the code of ethics, the rights and the privileges had differed between the educated and the uneducated. Both have tried to maintain separate methods of socialization, communication alliances and codes of behaviour. In order to safeguard the increasing exploitation and repression, the uneducated remain inobstrusive whereas the educated have both consciously and unconsciously evolved methods to improve the educational standards to become powerful both economically and politically respectively. Further, historical growth of higher education in India centred around state capitals and industrial and trade cities. In this sense, higher education tended to get associated with urban living and has acted as a deterrent to the rural men and women to return to their soil after higher education. This process essentially uprooted the rural elite from their mooring and resulted in higher concentration of educated persons in urban environment. Spread of higher education in rural and far-flung areas, in spite of high unemployment, suffers due to lack of good teachers as even the rural elites do not want to teach in these institutions. In this way we have a few urban based high quality institutions of excellence and a large number of low quality institutions of higher learning. It is succinctly described in the recent report by University Grants Commission while highlighting the major weakness of the higher education system in India.

> "The system maintains a set of double standards. A small minority of educational institutions at all levels is of good quality and compares favourably with those in developed countries. But access to them is selective and is mostly availed of by the top social groups, either because they can afford the costs involved or because they show merit which, on the basis of the existing methods of selection, show a higher correlation with social status. But this core of good

institutions where although there is open-door access, the standards are poor. Consequently it is in these institutions that the large majority of the people including the weaker sections receive their education. This dualism leads to undesirable social segregation and to a perpetuation and strengthening of inegalitarian trends in our society" (quoted from IGN Open University Project Report, 1985 : 8).

Communication Scenario and Choice of Technology

As soon as one departs from conventional face-to-face teaching, one is faced with many technologies viz., satellite, television, radio, computers and telephones. It is by choosing judiciously among the technologies available and by organizing the receiving end and keeping the cultural context in mind, that one can optimize the benefits to higher education.

India is the world's largest film producing country today (more than 800 feature films were produced in 1984). It can boast of one of world's largest radio and TV networks. (The country has about 180 TV transmitters and 100 radio stations). Technically, both radio and television are covering the entire country by their respective signals. An inexpensive medium-wave transistor helps connect the owner with the rest of the world. Exact number of radios is not known, but it is estimated to be around 40-50 million, keeping in view the life of a radio, about 10 per cent would be non-functional at any given time. With all these reductions in the total availability of the radio there would be one radio for every five households in the country (Misra, 1983). The same cannot be said of television and cinema halls which are clustered around urban centres. Right now, there is not even one television per thirty households. The cinema seat occupancy per thousand is also very low. The computer and related technologies have just begun to appear in elite institutions of higher education for large scale use by the students.

At present the University Grants Commission (UGC) is telecasting 'enrichment' programmes via INSAT-1B to all the transmitters which rebroadcast these programmes in their areas of coverage. In fact, more homes than colleges receive these programmes. This is one example of educational telecasting being highly dependent on time on the local transmitters. As the need for educational telecasting grows, particularly in the evening hours, time on the local transmitters will not be available. This would entail a separate transmitter network for higher education telecasting. However, desirable this may be, resource constraints simply will not permit such a huge investment in educational telecasting. The only alternative to this is direct broadcasting via satellite.

The institutions of higher education and open university study centres co-located with these institutions are likely to be dispersed and few in number. It would be very expensive to cover these with a separate transmitter network. Direct reception of programmes from the satellite will obviate the need for a transmitter network. Also a dedicated channel for higher education broadcasting will afford flexibility in programme scheduling. In this way, it is possible to provide experiences that cannot be obtained from textbooks : such as, live coverage of a one-shot surgical operation or a guided tour of a fast breeder-reactor. This can be accomplished through transportable uplinks. We should be aware of these possibilities and the opportunities afforded by one of the four S-Band direct broadcasting transponders to be made available on-board INSAT-II spacecraft in the 1990's time frame.

Radio is suitable for lectures, and the receivers being inexpensive, access for most students is possible. But countrywide reach, using a centrally located high-power transmitter, is ruled out. The All-India Radio is planning to set up a high-power national transmitter in Nagpur. But time on this transmitter is unlikely to be available for any educational broadcasting leave alone higher education. Therefore, for national coverage, quasi-direct sound broadcasting via satellite seems an obvious solution. This system, which is relatively new, is being studied and will be ready for implementation by 1990 or earlier. It would use inexpensive receivers with one meter antennae.

The use of Video Cassette Recorders (VCRs) is another example of useful technology for higher education. These VCRs located in an open university centre, or other institution of higher learning can be used for time-shifting the broadcast programme. They can also be used to view and distribute taped programmes in the non-broadcast mode. Thus, VCR's can play a useful role in providing flexibility in learning through television.

The telephone system in India has a very narrow base. Confined mostly to the rich, and government officials, it is mainly used for personal, business and administrative communications. An attempt should now be made to integrate the telephone into the educational system. Telephones should be made available at the study centres where tutors are available so that students can call up and clear their doubts about the materials they are studying. With electronic exchanges, even 'conference' calls can be made where four or five persons can simultaneously contact a tutor.

The foregoing analysis clearly indicates that extensive use of communication technologies at the individual level would be possible by radio, but if other audio-visual media are to be used for higher education, it should be considered under the institutional framework, given the cost and other logistic and infrastructural requirements. Otherwise, the use of audio-visual media will not achieve the intended goals. For example, INSAT television hour for college students today is viewed mostly at homes by non-college students as not even 3 per cent of colleges have more than one TV receiver to view these programmes. Can this kind of situation in any way, reduce the increasing disparity between the educated and the uneducated and between elite institutions and other institutions?

An evaluative study conducted to measure the educational effects of distance learning in higher education through APPLE satellite in 1983 indicated that television if used appropriately, can help bridge the knowledge gap between the students of elite and non-elite institutions (Agrawal, 1983). This a significant finding as it shows how an appropriate use of technology can be utilized in effective manner for improving the quality of education in an institutional framework.

Import Technology not Culture

Quite often in the past, along with the importation of technology, the inherent value system was also imported. This situation is well-known to the educationists who have witnessed the wholesale adoption of British education in terms of management, growth and development of academic disciplines. Even today, after almost four decades of India's independence, no major dents have been made in the functioning of colleges and universities. One is worried whether the same would happen with the communication technologies. The recent efforts made to provide higher education outside the classroom once again fall prey to the British model of open education. The use of TV, though intended to provide culturally compatible images, due to lack of software, has fallen into the same trap of larger scale import of educational programmes. Unless a conscious effort is made to use these technologies within the cultural framework, it will continue to perpetuate the age old intellectual slavishness and produce professionals who will look outside India for their intellectual fulfilment. What has been argued and has been well established by other studies, is that until and unless planning for academic input and other software areas precede the introduction of hardware the existing situation cannot be altered.

An equally important issue relates to the question of sender's approach versus receiver's approach in the use of technologies for higher education. As it stands today, government-owned media organizations, though very well-meaning, have followed a path in which they are through with the responsibility once a programme is transmitted, a plan is executed, and an experiment is successfully completed. This approach has essentially created a situation, in which the viewer, the listener, and the user remains in oblivion. This approach needs to be drastically altered so that the receiver could have some way to ensure access to the information and could help determine the needs to be catered for. This calls for means of access at college and university level for optimal use of even existing communication technologies.

Concluding Question

There are some questions that ought to be raised : Whether to use communication technologies for higher education? Is there a political will to enhance educational access in order to democratize it to achieve nationally defined goals? In order to answer these questions, it is equally important to ask whether the five thousand year old hegemony of the rich and the educated elite over the poor can be destroyed by such technological intervention. It is argued that without basic structural changes in the society and in the method of imparting and testing of knowledge, we would achieve very little. These questions must be squarely tackled if the new communication technologies are to be meaningfully integrated in order to improve the quality of higher education.

REFERENCES

Agrawal, Binod C. (1983). *Educational Impact of Distance Learning : An Evaluation of Telesymposium via APPLE on Satellite Communications*. Ahmedabad : Space Applications Centre.

Dholakia, Bakul H. (1978). *Changing Structure of Indian Economy*. Ahmedabad : Indian Institute of Management.

Indira Gandhi National Open University (1985). Indira Gandhi National Open University—Project Report. New Delhi : Educational Consultants India Ltd.

Misra, Sunil (1983). Radio as a Vehicle for Development. *Social Change*, Vol. 13(4) : pp. 19-22.

Ojha, P.D. (1971). A Configuration of Indian Poverty. In *Challenge of Poverty in India*. A.J. Fonseca (ed). Delhi : Vikas Publications.

3

EDUCATION AND SOCIO-CULTURAL IMPLICATIONS OF SATELLITE COMMUNICATION

Some Observations

BINOD C. AGRAWAL

INTRODUCTION

AFTER THE Second World War, with few exceptions, most of the countries of Asia had to meet the challenges of growing demand for education. During the same period one observed remarkable human achievements in the field of science and technology. The development of satellite technology is one such achievement which led to the revolutionary changes in the field of communication, telecommunication, broadcasting, telecasting and education. It has created immense new possibilities through which systems of communication will be created and operated. Speed and accuracy is the hallmark of this technology. The multinational electronic companies and international agencies are pushing the idea that communication is a key to development and education of the so called 'developing countries'. The advance technology of satellite has the capacity to neutralize distance disadvantages between rural and urban areas. It has the ability to make geographic boundaries irrelevant. These possibilities, if considered, in the framework of monolingual countries of Asia, could be a boon for development and education. But the same can not be said about multi-lingual and multi-cultural countries of Asia.

My effort in this paper is to examine some of the major socio-cultural implications of satellite communication for education in the context of Asia. While doing so, I would like to describe and analyse several evaluative studies conducted for measuring the effectiveness of satellite communication in education. My major data base will be from India as I have been involved in the experiments related to the applications of satellite communication for education including teachers' training. Within this context it is important to make a distinction between two concepts often used while discussing the use of satellite for education. These are 'enrichment' and syllabus based educational programmes. I thought it important as it will throw some light while discussing socio-cultural implications of satellite for education in Asia.

Educational Needs in the Developing Countries

Most of the Asian countries including India by any yard stick are 'developing countries', if education is one of the indicators for measuring development. Given the size of some of the Asian countries and population there is no way that the conventional system can meet the growing demands of schools to provide elementary education to all which is a constitutional requirement in some of these countries. In India, for example, the educational planners like those in other countries of Asia thought of using 'communication technology' to bridge the increasing educational gap with the help of satellite, assuming that it will multiply information. Let me quote India's founding father of space programme, Dr. Vikram Sarabhai who believed that :

> "In any developing country, one of the prime ingredients of development is the dissemination of information : information about new fertilizers, seeds, insecticides, cropping patterns, new technology, new findings and discoveries in all fields, new goods and services, new living patterns, etc. The process of education is basically related to an information dissemination/transfer process. For the rapid and sustained growth of developing countries, the urgent need to disseminate information to the masses is obvious. Mass media are clearly the main component in this system of information transfer." (Sarabhai 1969 : 5).

It is in this environment of urgency that satellite was thought to be an important tool for accelerating the process of education in India though adopted only after careful experimentation. Since then a number of Asian countries have been utilizing or plan to utilize satellite for education to the masses who otherwise would not get an opportunity of becoming educated (Alfian and Chu 1981). Some of the educational needs that can be met by satellite are :

(i) an uniform and standard education for a large number of students in a short period;
(ii) updating of knowledge base of both teachers and students;
(iii) reduction in the cost of education;

(iv) equal access of educational opportunities to all social classes;
(v) help enrich the students' educational experiences by expanding their horizon;
(vi) training of teachers, and
(vii) creating a sense of belonging to the nation.

It may by pointed out that most of these needs can be met through conventional mass media also. But two things which are unique to satellite are its capacity to cover a large area in real time and its neutrality to distance. So it is possible to have a common experience otherwise not possible through conventional media. Keeping these advantages in view the educational planners of India opted to "create a dedicated satellite system for educational needs in the long term" (National Policy on Education 1986 : 181).

SITE to INSAT for Education

In the history of satellite communication, SITE remains the world's largest techno-social experiment in education at the primary school level and for teachers' training (Agrawal, 1981). Education was one among many objectives of SITE. School children of 2330 backward villages primarily of rural origin and poor socio-economic background watched 'enrichment' television programmes for about 22-1/2 minutes while sitting in their classrooms or in the village community halls. The target audience of these television programmes were 5 to 11 years old school children of both sexes, studying in grades I to V. In SITE, about 38 per cent of total telecast time of four hours was devoted to educational television. Several evaluation studies were conducted to measure the impact of television on school children. Also some efforts were made to analyse the educational and societal implications of the introduction of satellite television for school education. Some of the salient findings are summarized here to draw major socio-cultural implications of satellite communication for education in the sub-continent and in other Asian countries.

Agrawal (1981) reported that both school children and teachers 'accepted' television and viewed it. But how far they thought of it as an educational aid is not known. No post-telecast discussions were held in majority of the schools thereby showing that television might have been viewed as 'little cinema' and not as an educational aid. At the same time, TV viewing led to increase in the general understanding and information seeking behaviour of the school children. Also TV viewing helped in the language development of the school children (Shukla and Kumar, 1977). The last observation is significant as all efforts were made to produce television programmes in four languages to cater the needs of the students of four linguistic regions. The same can be said about teachers' training.

> "Statistically significant gain was found in science knowledge content of the trainees as a result of multi-media package training. Most teachers felt that the training was useful. They also found that TV rather than radio was preferred for the training" (Agrawal 1981 : Summary).

What is the most significant aspect of SITE which is generally glossed over is the fact that ATS-6 satellite was only used for 12.5 per cent of the total time for national telecast for all the 2230 SITE villages. The remaining satellite time was shared by four linguistic regions. For example, 90 minutes of school telecast time was shared by four linguistic regions. In other words, the unique potential of the satellite was not fully used. Instead, it acted as a sequential transmitter and catered to the needs of each specific linguistic region separately even though centralized telecast approach was followed. Given the linguistic and cultural multiplicity in India, the satellite could not be used as a large scale 'message multiplier', across the nation, instead, it acted as an efficient delivery system for reaching to the remote areas of a linguistic region. The SITE experience clearly indicated that the future satellite based television system will not be used as in other countries of Asia where it is utilized for nation-wide telecast in a single language mode.

After SITE, an operational system of satellite became a reality for India. The Indian National Satellite (INSAT) is now being used for the education of school children and for higher education. The mode of satellite transmission remained more or less same as during SITE on a time sharing basis by various linguistic regions for school telecast. Cultural factors imposed on technology could not be solved even in the operational phase of the INSAT though it is being utilized for nation-wide telecast of higher education programmes in single language mode.

Some soul searching on the part of technologists and planners is needed to alter the present method of satellite use especially for education or redefine the technical configuration of the satellite to meet the cultural needs.

Linguistic Conflicts and Educational Homogenization

Centralised, top-down planning is essential for satellite telecasting. A single television programme conceived and produced at any place can be viewed by the entire globe by an appropriate technical configuration through satellites. International sports and other events are regularly telecast in this mode. A similar approach is being followed in India both for entertainment, sports and education.

The best example of this kind of educational telecast is 'Country-wide Classroom' in India. Twice for an hour on every working day of the week, the enrichment educational television programmes are telecast for the undergraduate students of some 5,000 colleges spread over the entire sub-continent of India. The language of the programme is English, though in most of the colleges and universities the medium of instruction is the language of the region which add up to more than fifteen in number. In the present circumstances, there is no plan to change this kind of telecast.

Research studies indicate that undergraduate students of various linguistic regions prefer to view 'Country-wide Classroom' TV programmes in the language in which they are being taught at the college level. (Agrawal, Aghi and Ramanathan 1986). Given the satellite configuration and present 'elitist policy' in this regard, the students, are forced to view television programmes in English. The choice of medium of English has forced the planners to opt for enrichment programmes instead of syllabus based programmes in most areas.

An even worse situation exists in case of primary school teachers who are being trained through television under new 'National Policy on Education 1986'. The programmes for training have been produced in one language (mostly Hindi and/or English). The teachers who know one of the fifteen languages are expected to learn from these television programmes after hearing a summary of the programme in their 'mother tongue'. One can illustrate several such examples to emphasize the point that satellite telecast in its present configuration is leading to high degree of non-comprehension, sense of imposition and serious linguistic conflicts among the learners. Apart from these problems, there are deeper political sensitivities and repercussions of this kind of telecast. While it is possible that satellite television may impart an uniform education it may lead to educational homogenization. In a country-wide telecast, it will not be possible to have a two-way communication for any clarification also. The net effect it seems will be one way transfer of information. It seems satellite television can, and will, provide 'accurate facts' and standardized 'knowledge' but will take away the differing view points, interactions and discussions at classroom and group levels.

Satellite Use for Technical Education

One of the interesting experiments conducted in India relates to use of APPLE (Ariane Passenger Payload Experiment) for giving a course aimed at providing advance course in satellite communications to engineering students of four colleges located several thousand kilometres away from each other. The 'TV Course' package consisted of two sets of material. These were : (a) lecture notes, and (b) video lectures to be telecast via APPLE satellite. In addition, two way voice link facility was made available for live discussion between students and lecturers who had originally prepared the lecture material. The four day course was attended by advanced students of engineering.

An evaluative study was conducted to measure the gain in knowledge as a result of TV viewing in the subject matter areas of the students coming from institutions having differing educational standards. It was observed that the pretest knowledge level in general was higher among the students coming from 'elite' institutions as compared to the students of 'normal' institutions. In the post test the knowledge gaps were bridged between the students of elite and normal institutions. As a result, they attained more or less similar knowledge level. Another interesting feature observed in the study was that students coming from the families of higher income group compared to lower income group gained more from the TV course regardless of their institutional affiliation. There seems to be some correlation between income and knowledge gained as a result of TV course.

The major conclusion originally drawn from the evaluation was that such a course helped bridge the knowledge gap between the elite and normal institutions. Hence, more such courses via satellite should be offered. However, one must not lose sight of the fact that it was a highly specialized course in which medium of instruction was English and the course was on a topic little known to the students. If the same course is telecast for all the science and engineering colleges, it may end-up transfering some 'facts' without providing any opportunity for interaction and discussion. Satellite communication in this respect creates a contradiction between 'learning' and 'transfer of facts' which needs to be carefully examined in the future.

Satellite the Message Multiplier without Access

There is no parallel in the history, the way television expanded in India in last five years. The slogan used during the expansion phase was 'transmitter a day'. In less than five years, India leap frogged from a handful of television transmitters located in few cosmopolitan cities to an impressive number of more than 200 television transmitters dotted all over the country. These transmitters are capable of receiving direct signals from

INSAT for relay to cover more than 70 per cent of India's population. Expansion here denoted 'message multiplication' of centrally produced programmes and 'signal reach' and not 'access'. The implication of this development assumes greater importance when a country is committed to using satellite for education. At present, the television access is limited to less than two per cent population in India mostly living in urban areas, thereby limiting the access of educational programmes to elite households. Technology is 'neutral' and it has helped to create viewing facilities for a large population. But lack of viewing facilities has limited its utility.

How Cost Effective is Satellite?

Except in early seventies when few economists raised questions on cost aspect of satellite not much efforts have been made to calculate the cost effectiveness of satellite use for education (Melzer 1974 and Dhawan, 1975). Recently Srivastava, (1987) made an earnest effort to calculate per hour per person receiving cost of television in India. He concluded that there will be reduction of cost as number of TV sets would increase in the country. In two countries like India and Indonesia, little comparative data are available to answer whether satellite for education is cost effective or not. There are indications that satellite can reduce direct communication costs if used in centralised mode. Some efforts are required to investigate this aspect of satellite as it directly related with the socio-economic and political factors of the country and other competing needs of communication.

Another dimension of cost relates to the software production and distribution of receive system for appropriate utilization. In the monolingual production, the involved production staff are able to take care of the cultural nuances and correct visual symbols. But in the case of these production meant for multi-lingual viewers greater care and research would be required to overcome these problems. Many think that it would increase the cost of production so much that it would not be cost effective. A more serious problem is the investments in the receive system by the individuals as a 'private cost' and by the government as 'public cost'. Some of these issues have been recently discussed by Bates (1987) in a draft paper which requires discussion at a larger forum. Comparative studies in this area are needed to determine the cost effectiveness of satellite communication for education.

Increased Social Inequality and Educational Gap

Major satellite related educational studies conducted in India provide some disquieting conclusions. Television viewing is creating information gap between owners and non-owners of television (Agrawal 1982). In case of higher education, use of English language for telecast will further create educational gulf between the students of poor and rich colleges until access to receive educational broadcast are created at all colleges. As indicated elsewhere, the satellite telecast will further accentuate the existing disparities (Agrawal 1987). Lack of community viewing facilities especially in rural schools and community halls is also accelerating information and knowledge gap between the elite and the poor students. Until this dimension is curbed the bliss of technology will create new social problems which will go against the cherished goals of equality in several Asian countries.

Increased Technological Dependency

At present, there are only six countries which can boast of having some of the technical capabilities required to launch a satellite though all of them are not at the same level of technological sophisticaton. Majority of satellite owning or building countries are the so called 'developed countries'. Though Asia does not lack this capacity, the magnitude and quantity of the satellite use remains limited except maybe in one country. Wherever it is being used, it is generally meant for national development and education. While it has increased both reach and access of information, it is gradually increasing technological dependency of the developing countries to developed countries. This process will continue and there is no method by which this can be reversed. It is, therefore, essential to discuss this vital techno-political issue in detail and its implications. Before the total information technology and information production/ generation capabilities are controlled by a few countries, it would be critical for the survival of the cultures and countries to have a firm grip on the situation to reverse the concentration of information 'power' and thereby knowledge in few hands.

Educational Invasion Beyond National Boundaries

The present trend in the educational broadcast is to import software from other countries as it is cheaper and easier to do so. Also lack of production facilities and trained human power do not permit many countries to have proper production facilities. The cost of production is also very high. So there is a tendency to import software. Once such a programme is telecast at the national level, as is the case in India for higher education, one is not sure whether the value system connected with the programme would not gradually creep in. All care has been taken while selecting 'foreign' programmes for telecast to avoid such problems. However observations indicated that the visuals used in the programmes are culture specific. There are two arguments in this connection. First, that such programmes provide visual feasts to the viewers and better understanding of cultural differences. Second, that it leads to a sense of inadequacy among the viewers. At present atleast there are no data to support or reject these views. Indications are available from several countries of South America, Asia and Africa about the educational invasion through mass media.

It seems to me that what centuries of colonial powers could not achieve through ruthless means is being done through slow but poisonous opiate of television pictures. It is this kind of process of cultural invasion that I am seriously concerned about as I see this as a slow method of inducing a new value system leading to destruction of the very fabric of the ancient civilizations of Asia. In more concrete terms, it is creating a 'world view' or 'consumerism' and 'selfcenterism'. The materialism of 'modern' tradition is making inroads in such a way that there will be no place for alternate thinking left for the human beings of Asia. Let us hope that the viewers of the educational programmes will be able to discern the differences.

Breaking of Intercultural Barriers

It is beyond doubt that there are going to be conflicts of interest which is apparent in case of India as a result of centralized monolingual satellite broadcasting. The opposite is equally true that a country of India's size and cultural heterogeneity now shares a common experience when a national event is telecast on TV whether celebration of Independence Day or a Cricket Match. In the field of educational broadcasting, this is even much more pronounced. The reason being that the entry knowledge level of the students watching these programmes happens to be more or less same. This provides an added advantage in breaking the intercultural barriers among those who are at the same level of socio-economic development. Given the cultural diversity and level of economic development in several countries of Asia, there is little exposure of the external world. Also there is no way to have direct contact with the outside world. It is here that the satellite permits visual experience in real time. It is a positive gain of the satellite communication which helps breaking intercultural barriers. Identifications of different cultures, style of living, world view, and religious beliefs are shared through satellite communication which will increase in the future leading to global understanding.

Blurring of National Boundaries of Education

Based on the experiences in India, in the use of 'foreign' programmes, it is safe to say that some of the educational programmes could be utilized by other countries of Asia and similarly, programmes can be exchanged for this purpose. If logically this idea is expended, it will clearly show a path for higher utilization of educational programmes in several countries of Asia especially in technical and medical fields. In scientific experimentation and vocational education such an effort might lead to blurring of the national boundaries. This is one area in which serious research efforts are required to evolve methods of programme production for its greater use at various levels. Specialised higher level courses meant for few participants in each country can take advantage of satellite based communication system.

Concluding Comments

So far I have tried to discuss both negative and positive socio-cultural implications of satellite communication vis-a-vis education. I have limited my observations to some selected variables and aspects. These observations were based on a limited research data. Given the importance of the topic in the global context some analyses related to communication technology, culture and education will be essential. Such an analysis will provide appropriate social direction for Asia and other developing countries. It will help take rational decision before opting for satellite to solve development and educational problems of many Asian countries.

REFERENCES

Agrawal, Binod C. (1987). Video Use in Distance Education : A South Asian Perspective. Paper presented at CIDA-AMIC Seminar on Training Needs in the Use of Media for Distance Education. AMIC Singapore, June 8—11, 1987.

Agrawal, Binod C. (1983). Educational Impact of Distance Learning : An Evaluation of Tele-symposium via APPLE on Satellite Communications. (Part I) Ahmedabad : Space Applications Centre.

Agrawal, Binod C. (1982). Satellite Communication Technology for Development : The Indian Scene. Paper presented at the 13th International Association for Mass Communication Research Conference Paris, September 6-10, 1982.

Agrawal, Binod C. (1981). *SITE Social Evaluation : Results, Experiences, and Implications*. Ahmedabad : Space Applications Centre.

Agrawal, Binod C., Mira, B. Aghi and Arundhati Ramanathan (eds) (1986). INSAT Pre-production Television Research for Higher Education : A Consolidated Report for UGC. Ahmebabad : DECU, ISRO.

Alfian and Godwin, C. Chu (eds) (1981). *Satellite Television in Indonesia*. Honolulu : East West Center Communication Institute.

Bates, A.W. (1987). The Use of Satellites for Education in Common wealth Countries : Policy Issues—first draft. Milton Keynes : Open University (xeroxed copy).

Dhawan, B.D. (1975). *Economics of TV for India.* New Delhi : S. Chand.

Melzer, Alexander (1974). The Social Use of India's Television Satellite : A Technology Assessment of the INSAT Proposal. Zurich : Centre for Economic Research, Swiss Federal Institute of Technology.

National Policy on Education (1986). *Programme of Action.* New Delhi : Government of India, Ministry of Human Resource Development, Department of Education.

Sarabhai, Vikram (1969). Television for Development. Paper presented at the Society for International Development Conference, New Delhi, November 14-17, 1969.

Shukla, Snehlata and Kuldip Kumar (1977) *SITE Impact Study on Children.* Bangalore : Indian Space Research Organisation.

Srivastava, U.K. (1987). National Cost of Television in India in the Year 2000 : Socio-economic and Political Implications and Issues. *Media Asia.* 14 (3) : 136—148.

4

INSAT PRE-PRODUCTION (FORMATIVE) TELEVISION RESEARCH FOR COUNTRYWIDE CLASSROOM

BINOD C. AGRAWAL, MIRA B. AGHI AND ARUNDHATI RAMANATHAN

INTRODUCTION

IT WAS in July 1983 that the University Grants Commission (UGC) decided to utilize a 'one hour' slot of transmission time on Indian National Satellite IB (INSAT-1B), for telecasting programmes for higher education. UGC after considerable thought, decided to undertake production of programmes immediately to overcome the problems of software and programme production. It was felt that materials produced abroad, as well as in India should be viewed, and suitable materials having educational value be selected. A special committee was set up in Jamia Millia Islamia, New Delhi which was assigned this responsibility. At this point, an initial decision that the programmes would be in simple English and would be directed to undergraduate students was also taken.

The main objective of the UGC in utilizing the satellite for higher education was to bring about an improvement in the quality of education. This was to be attempted by exposing students to television programmes and information which they would normally have no access to, stimulate them to think, and improve the overall quality of education. It was at this stage that the Research Advisory Committee (RAC) discussed in detail the feasibility of conducting a number of pre-production or 'formative researches'.

Pretesting : Its Importance in Communication Research

According to Palmer, (1972 : 165)* formative research is "designed to help improve the quality of educational products and practices during the

* Palmer, E.L. (1972) Formative Research in Educational Television Production : The Experience of the Children's Television Workshop. In : *Quality in Instructional Television* by Wilbur Schram (ed). Honolulu : The University Press of Hawaii.

actual course of their development". Most of the time one finds communicators producing information laden programmes without really having sufficient knowledge about the target groups who are actually going to view it. The programmes produced are usually based on their professional expertise personal judgement, intuition and preconceived ideas. Pretesting is one such exercise which helps in avoiding failures after the investment of precious production inputs. It helps in providing a feedback on the audience reaction, both quantitative and qualitative on various aspects of television programme production. The results obtained are an important input found useful before one embarks upon large scale production and use of a particular medium. The objectives set by UGC for undertaking such an exercise was to find out the level of student comprehension, especially of the programmes produced abroad (referred to as foreign programme). It was also designed to yield data on the social profile of undergraduate students, including their level of English comprehension, media exposure, and educational and informational needs. In addition pretesting would throw light on the infrastructure facilities available in the colleges for viewing TV like electricity, hall/classroom and viewing condition.

The Research Advisory Committee (RAC) proposed to pretest a set of selected programmes in six centres from six regions of the country. This was mainly with the idea of obtaining a comprehensive picture of the reactions of our undergraduate students on the television programmes going to be telecast. The research design was to be experimental, where two sets of programmes would be used, one as originally produced in English abroad and the second set with an intervention for the same programme. Much earlier in the discussion between the educationists and UGC experts, it was suggested that programmes produced abroad can also be meaningfully telecast provided these programmes are introduced by Indian professors with Indian illustrations. This approach was to be followed in all the foreign programmes.

The Indian professor who introduced these programmes were referred to as 'facilitators'. The effectiveness of this approach was to be studied.

Accordingly it was considered essential to pretest the foreign programmes 'with a facilitator and without the facilitator'.

Five major regions or states where logistic support would be available were to be identified. Purposive sampling in view of the individual variables and locational conditions was to be considered while conducting the pretesting. Both observational and recall data was to be collected (recall data through individual interviews and with the help of a questionnaire in a group situation and observational data by the researchers present during the actual pretesting sessions).

After the acceptance of the proposal, a set of six programmes, three produced abroad and three in India were selected as a representative sample of the programmes for pretesting. After carefully viewing the programmes along with the subject matter specialists, the questionnaires were developed which consisted of the pre and post-test questions in English for each of the programmes.

Instrument Pretesting

Before actually using the questionnaires in the pretesting exercise, it was felt important to field test them in one of the locations. The same was done in Ahmedabad, at Space Applications Centre with a group of 35 students who had come for a sports camp from all over the state. The pretesting was conducted in the same manner as it would be done during actual TV programme pretesting at each region. The only difference was that during analysis while going through the completed questionnaires the researcher's focus was on the comprehension of the questions and relevance of answers rather than the correctness of the answers. The questionnaires in the light of the results were then modified.

Project Leader's Workshop

At this stage, it was considered important to hold a workshop of all the individual project leaders and members of the Research Programme Advisory Committee to discuss operational details of the pretest design and execution. The four major aims of holding the workshop were :

(a) to familiarise the project leaders and coordinators with the task of pretesting;
(b) to finalise the set of instruments for pretesting; and
(c) to know each of the project leaders and the overall goal of the project.

The instrument developed earlier for this pretesting was distributed in the Workshop. The first day was mostly devoted towards discussing the scope of INSAT television for higher education and its planning.

Previewing each of the six programmes, three foreign and three Indian and thereafter discussing the instruments in light of the observation was another major activity carried out on the subsequent days. It was here that the final version of the questionnaires emerged. The methodological strategy too was finalised and the logistics worked out keeping in mind the location of each centre. After the workshop half inch VHS tapes were prepared for each of the six regions.

The following pages record how the pretesting was actually conducted by individual project leaders and the kind of experiences and insights that have emerged from the programme pretesting.

METHODOLOGICAL STRATEGY FOR PRETESTING

While presenting the methodological strategy for pretesting, our effort will be to document the methods and techniques that were followed for this study. This is what emerged from the initial research proposal, instrument pretesting, discussions during the three days workshop, and the actual procedures that individual project leaders had to adapt to, in response to the local situations. As mentioned earlier, the design conceived in the initial proposal was as given below in the pretest frame work Table 4.1.

Table 4.1 : Number of Pretest Location and Regions Suggested.

Sr. No.	*Module Type*	*No. of pretest locations*	*No. of Regions covered*
1.	Module with facilitator	Ten	Five
2.	Module without facilitator	Ten	Five

Sampling

For this study, a two stage sampling procedure was to be followed. The first stage being, the selection of an university from a region, for which the country was divided into five regions namely : (a) Northern region (Uttar Pradesh and Delhi); (b) North Eastern region (c) Southern region (Tamil Nadu, Karnataka and Andhra Pradesh; (d) Western region (Maharashtra and Gujarat), and (e) Eastern region (Orissa). At the second stage two institutions from the three types of institutions as indicated in Table 4.2 were to be selected.

Table 4.2 : Sample Distribution According to Institutions

Sr. No.	*Batch*	*Medium of instruction*	*Sample Size*	*Male/Female*
1.	Institution 1	English	30	Proportional
2.	Institution 2	Regional Language amd English	30	Proportional
3.	Institution 3	Regional Language	30	Proportional

After the three day workshop some changes did come about in the procedure suggested, although not of a very basic nature. With the constraint on time and money the pretesting was to be restricted to six states, namely, Andhra Pradesh, Gujarat, Karnataka, Maharashtra, Uttar Pradesh and Meghalaya. Pretesting in and around one university in each of these states was planned, the universities being, Hyderabad (Osmania University), Ahmedabad (Gujarat University), Bangalore (Bangalore University), Pune (Poona University), Gorakhpur (Gorakhpur University), and Shillong (North Eastern Hill University). Pretesting in each university involved selection of four colleges where medium of instruction was both English and the regional language. Within each college two groups of students were selected. The size of each group being between 30-50, with care being taken to see that the size did not fall below 30 even after allowing for dropouts. The total sample size in each sector ranged, therefore, between 240-400 (i.e. 30×2×4 to 50×2×4), except Hyderabad where it was 118 (See Table 4.3).

Table 4.3 : Pretest Sample Size by University

	Ahmebabad	*Bangalore*	*Gorakhpur*	*Pune*	*Hyderabad*
Rural	118	98	110	182	27
Urban	215	216	187	189	91
Total	333	314	297	371	118

The sample selection procedure was done keeping four background variables of the respondents in mind, (a) Subject or discipline, (b) Sex male/female, (c) Location of the college-urban area/rural area, and (d) Year of study in college—first/second/third year. The priority alloted to each of these variables was in the order of listing.

The rationale for considering these four variables while drawing the sample was that the programmes both to be bought from abroad and the indigenously produced, were going to be of "general education and enrichment type". They were to be directed at undergraduate college students all streams. Also the 5000 odd colleges where these programmes were to be viewed were located both in rural and urban areas. The stress, therefore, was to be able to achieve a sample as representative as possible. The two matched groups in each college drawn for pretesting were :

Group 1 : Those viewing foreign programmes with facilitator;
Group 2 : Those viewing foreign programmes without facilitator.

Close observation at the Table 4.3 reveals that the sample size finalized before the execution of the pretesting could not be adhered to. A variety of reasons each applicable to a different location can be stated. They were :

1. Non-availability of students because of prevailing unrest in the city (Hyderabad);
2. Examinations were not held as per schedule and so reopening of the new academic year created problem (Gorakhpur);
3. Girls in rural and urban areas but particularly in the rural areas, did not want to sit for the afternoon session because of lack of adequate transport facilities to return home. (Ahmedabad);
4. Variations in the degrees of motivation among the volunteer students also added to the problem. The motivation level did not always remain high;
5. Non-science and students not fluent with English seemed to get bored quickly and leave in between a session;
6. Many a times students would leave their questionnaires unfilled which were eventually dropped from the sample; and
7. Electricity failure during a number of sessions in rural areas hindered data collection (Pune).

Method of Data Collection

A mixed group of 30 to 50 students were selected for programme viewing. If there were students other than the selected sample who wanted to view the programmes they were allowed to do so. Each college was visited on two days. The programmes were shown to the groups in the order indicated below :

	Group-1	*Group-2*
First Day	Foreign Programme without facilitator	Foreign programme with facilitator
Second Day	Indian Programme	Indian Programme

Each group thus viewed both the foreign and the Indian programmes. If there arose a fear of contamination between the two groups on the first day, both the groups were shown the foreign programmes on the first day and on the second day the groups were shown Indian programmes.

For each programme viewing session the actual method followed is indicated below in the sequence it was done.

1. Introduction by project leader.
2. Answering the student response sheet and general questionnaire.
3. Filling of the pre-programme questionnaire.
4. Filling of the post-programme viewing questionnaire.
5. Viewing of programme.
6. A brief group discussion on the programme.
7. Filling the general questionnaire after viewing all the programme in one session.

Steps three, four, five and six repeated for every programme shown, while steps one, two and seven only once in every session.

In order to maintain uniformity in the data it was considered most desirable that an uniform method must be followed everywhere, during the data collection phase. Accordingly, the project leaders were requested to follow the set of instruction. First being the introduction, second being the observational data to be collected, third the method of analysis and fourth the budget schedule of pretesting. Each of these instructions were cyclostyled and given to each of the project leaders originally prepared by Dr. R. Amritawalli after the workshop.

Instruction to Students

The students were told that the U.G.C. plans to have regular telecasts for students like them all over India. Programmes already available outside India, and those produced in India for this purpose, both will be telecast. They should watch carefully and help determine if the programmes that are going to be shown are suitable to their needs and also suggest changes. This was not going to be an examination. Their performance was not an issue, rather their help was sought in programme production. They must answer each question in English preferably or in their regional language.

Observational Data

Each project leader had a research assistant taking down observational notes. Observational sheets would be used to ensure uniformity. Points to note were eye movements, evidence of attentiveness, excitement such as speaking out loud involuntarily drawing the attention of a neighbour etc. This data were felt particularly important for the Indian programmes, as the suggestions and opinions could be incorporated in future programme production. The group discussions planned at the end of each session was with the idea of extracting data on programme production quality, their strategies of communication and format. The latter being of particular importance to the programmes with a facilitator.

Analysis

The analysis was done at two levels. First, at each of the individual locations by the project leaders and second, by the project coordinators.

Budget

The budget estimates as discussed in the workshop for each pretesting centre is provided in the appendix. Our experience indicated that though there were minor variations in the expenditure from one location to another the overall cost did not exceed the stipulated funds though time schedule of the pretesting could not be adhered to, due to several reasons. Reports from individual project leaders came on different dates in different formats. Hence it was difficult to bring out a consolidated report immediately. Though we had immediate feedback on student reactions on programmes pretested in Shillong, an edited report was not made available by the project leader leading to further delay in preparation of this report.

PRETEST RESULTS AND PRODUCTION IMPLICATIONS

In this Section an attempt has been made to synthesize the results of individual programme pretests, conducted in different linguistic locations. The aim in doing so, is to provide a broad understanding as to how the undergraduate students responded in terms of their comprehension of English programmes their needs and expectations. We have interpreted some of the findings for the purpose of programme production, and a qualitative analyses has been attempted in the process. The aim being that of facilitating its utilization in future production. Also efforts have been made to bring out the salient aspects related to foreign and Indian programmes in terms of content presentation techniques, language, and other important aesthetic aspects.

Social Profile of the Undergraduate Students

The social profile of the students drawn for the sample mainly provides a picture of the degree of TV exposure the undergraduate students have had, their opinions and views on what topics they would like programmes to be made, where they would want to watch these, and finally their language preferences.

An estimated total of 68.5 per cent of students seem to be exposed to television. All the percentages provided here have been estimated from the individual reports. Hence no tables have been provided. Although the pretesting in rural areas was restricted to colleges situated around the periphery of the city, the amount of media exposure seems to be pretty high. About 42.5 per cent of the students mentioned that they had a television set at home. This high percentage of ownership explains more than two thirds of the students exposure, though this aggregate includes TV viewers of varying degrees. A large number, as much as 89.3 per cent seemed to believe that television can be used for learning, out of which 67.7 per cent felt that TV should be used for general education; while 26.5 per cent wanted syllabus based programmes. About 63.1 per cent indicated that they would like to watch these programmes in college while 32.3 per cent wanted to view it elsewhere, meaning at home, community place, and clubs. From the foregoing analysis it is apparent that television is not unfamiliar for a large majority of students, and is positively associated with learning. The important issue that needs to be discussed is as to how this facility can be provided for large scale viewing within the college and within the existing time table.

Language Preference

There is a distinct difference in language preference for TV programmes between the five locations. While in Ahmedabad and Gorakhpur, a majority have shown their preference for Gujarati and Hindi programmes respectively, those in Bangalore, Pune and Hyderabad have indicated their first preference for English programmes. Ahmedabad audiences have indicated Hindi language as a second preference, while Gorakhpur indicate English. The pattern in Bangalore, Pune and Hyderbad is opposite to this. Here as second preference they would like to view programmes in their regional language. However, a small group of students everywhere have shown their preference for programmes in English and their respective regional languages. Keeping in view the policy of telecasting only programmes in English, some rethinking would be required in light of the above analyses.

Programme Needs

Students have shown a very broad spectrum of areas to be covered within the higher education telecast. Broadly they could be categoried as subject related topics. International events, language learning (specially English) General Knowledge, and entertainment. Under subject related topics, a long test ranging from literature, social sciences, to science and law have been indicated. Few wanted that current affairs and international events should be covered, which is generally being covered in the evening telecast. Special mention has been made of covering programmes aimed at teaching English language. Sports and quiz programmes were also mentioned by a large majority of students. Interest to view experts discussing new areas of research programme religion on industry and health were also indicated by the students.

Programme Specific Results

As indicated in the earlier section two sets of programmes were pre-tested, one, those produced abroad, and two, those produced within the country. In order to measure the responses of these two kinds of programmes separate analysis of each of these two types of programmes are presented here.

Foreign Programmes

Ascent of Man

The overall picture that emerges after the viewing of 'Ascent of Man' is that it is a beautiful visual feast but contributes little to comprehension of subject matter. The visuals help in holding the attention, but due to lack of language comprehension, (the commentary being in English) students in all the five locations reported the programme to be long and boring. Most students clearly stated that it was the English accent of the narrator which hindered the level of comprehension. This feeling was not only restricted to students from rural backgrounds but was also felt among English medium students, although they reported high comprehension and showed more knowledge gain, compared to other groups.

The presence of the narrator (Bronowski) on the screen too, was not appreciated. There is a clear indication that Bronowski was perceived as a teacher/lecturer and thereby the students tended to lose interest in the programme.

In Pune and Ahmedabad, it seems that television viewing as far as possible should create non-teaching climate for learning. Serious efforts are required to test the utility of such a format for future production of such programmes. The technique of introducing a facilitator to help the students in comprehension was generally liked by the viewers especially in

Ahmedabad, Bangalore and Gorakhpur. However, this in no way helped the students to improve the understanding of the subject matter. It is possible that the duration of the programme being 50 minutes might have led to this. It is supported by another comment by students of Gorakhpur, who thought that for the programme to be successful there should be a 'facilitator'. Further, it was commented that the 'facilitator' should use very simple English or if possible the regional language to foster greater comprehension.

This calls for a very serious reconsideration of the policy on the use of English in programme production, and the use of new technologies for solving such an issue like single video, multiple audio.

Magnetism

The educational level of this programme in almost all the locations was considered to be below college level. This helped students from both urban and rural colleges to hold their interest and to comprehend the content of the programme.

Use of the demonstration technique was liked by the students as they thought it helped them in understanding the concepts presented. The English accent of the lecturer was not comprehended fully by the students, although some indicated that the vocabulary used was simple. In Ahmedabad and Pune, students had difficulty in following the programme both in urban and rural areas due to the pronunciation of the lecturer.

On the whole, the facilitator played a positive role in helping the students to comprehend the content and also in preparing the students to receive the content to be presented. This was especially emphasized in Gorakhpur. Urban English medium students seemed to gain the maximum, while the rural 'without facilitator' groups showed minimum gains. It was found that post test scores in all groups were higher, thereby showing some gains after viewing the programme. In Bangalore the students were puzzled by the question put by the facilitator in the programme. This seemed to have distracted their attention. Another observation mentioned was that the appearance of the facilitator after the programme credits was of no great relevance because, as soon as the credits or titles started appearing on the screen, the students began to withdraw both physically and mentally. Care ought to be taken to see that the facilitator should come in before the credits appear.

The results of this programme indicates that to ensure greater learning, it would be advisable to move from known simple concepts to unknown complex concepts even in the case of television enrichment programmes. In such a situation language also may not pose to be a very serious barrier. Demonstration format would further enhance learning as it has been found to be a desirable method of presentation in the learning process.

Science students comprehended the programme better than the non-science students, and the urban students comprehended better than rural students. An extreme situation was observed in Ahmedabad rural colleges where comprehension was "almost nil".

Tomorrow's Energy

This programme was considered informative, interesting and easy to understand. It was because of these reasons that the programme seemed to hold the attention of the viewers. The documentary technique followed in the programme was preferred to the lecture method. Though the English language was said to be the chief reason for non-comprehension, it was felt that, of the three programmes, the pronunciation of the commentator in this programme was most comprehensible. It was further suggested that narration at slower pace and clearer diction would help in understanding the programme better. This can be said for almost all the programmes.

Based on the analyses it would be recommended that programmes of this kind should be selected for telecast. Three factors play an important role in high comprehension and attention. These are its documentary format which is fairly familiar to cinema viewers, its theme or topic of current interest and slow pace of background commentary.

The Foreign Programmes—A Comparison

It seems that the students conceptually separate instructional programmes from general television programme which is much closer to the existing notion about cinema. Television viewing is closer to cinema viewing, and therefore, is not expected to discuss any serious class room related instructional material. However, if viewed as a classroom instruction it can have desirable effects in terms of learning through television.

A comparison of the three foreign programmes though limited, supports this view. 'Tomorrow's Energy' ranked high as an inspiring programme and managed to maintain interest. The information content was also said to be valued by the students of Ahmedabad, Gorakhpur and Pune. With regard to vocabulary again 'Tomorrow's Engery' was related as having the simplest vocabulary in Ahmedabad and Bangalore, while

Gorakhpur rated 'Ascent of Man' high on vocabulary. In Pune the picture was slightly different, namely, urban and rural girls rated 'Magnetism' high while rural boys rated 'Tomorrow's Energy' high. When asked to rate the most inspiring programme and programme giving valuable information 'Tomorrow's Energy' was rated high by students of Ahmedabad, Gorakhpur and Pune. Between the other two programmes namely, 'Ascent of Man' and 'Magnetism' one cannot clearly say which was rated second because both were rated second an equal number of times.

A closer look reveals that on the whole 'Tomorrow's Energy' was liked best by a majority of the students. The programme format, music, language, length or duration, topic or theme, all helped in making it an interesting programmes. Also this programme dealt much less with facts and technicalities. The topic too, was a current issue requiring more general knowledge rather than previous knowledge for its comprehension.

Indian Programmes

Introduction to Computers

A majority of students were found to gain at least some understanding of computers after viewing the programme. The technique of recapitulation, summarizing and captioning used in the programme, was indicated as very helpful for comprehension. A suggestion was made here of including, if possible a summary in the regional language. Students of Bangalore and Ahmedabad commented that they found this programme interesting and rated it as good. Pune students mentioned that the music and clear visuals helped them in holding their attention.

Regarding language, many students indicated that the level of English was beyond their comprehension. This along with the novelty of the information presented, was mentioned as a cause for their low scores on the post-tests. Urban, Science English medium students seemed to comprehend the best.

The pace of narration and visuals was indicated as high by the students from rural and urban areas of Bangalore, Pune and Ahmedabad. The amount of information or the information load was mentioned as being very high. Students from some locations suggested that it could be broken down into two programmes. Along with the amount of information, a content expert in one of the locations revealed that the difficulty level of the programme and questionnaire was high, and this coupled with little previous knowledge hindered comprehension.

The conclusions that emerge from a close examination of the findings are that while introducing a novel concept like computers, serious efforts should be made to use self explanatory visuals as far as possible. At the same time the verbal content should be in simple language, clear diction and with an optimal number of repititions. The visuals and the commentary should move at the right pace (slower than what it is at present) to aid comprehension. The information load in quantity and the difficulty levels needs to be reduced.

Very little research exists on the pace of narration, to be followed in the documentary format. Given the heterogeneous character of the students and the expected learning outcomes from the viewing, it necessitates serious research efforts in the programme production phase, to decide the 'right speed'. It is especially important because the topics covered are to be viewed by students of all streams, from both rural and urban areas and with different degrees of media exposure.

Flower

The initial response to this programme was that of high enthusiasm but soon this gots replaced with bored expressions due to the presentation of technical details. Music and captions did seem appropriate, but the programme on the whole was found to be pretty difficult because of the use of Latin names.

A few students did suggest the use of location names so as to aid identification. Students of Pune suggested that a brief summary at the beginning would help an average non-specialist student. Going by the scores, botany and science students seemed to have liked and understood the programme better than arts students. Urban students seemed to follow better, compared to other groups. In Ahmedabad, it was observed that urban, non-science Gujarati medium students showed a high score on the pre-tests while science English medium students did better on the post-tests. Therefore, one can say that although previous knowledge was high among non-science Gujarati medium students the English medium science students gained more, because they comprehended the language of the programme better.

Some students of Bangalore have indicated that the visuals many a time, did not move in pace with the commentary. This confused the viewers. Caution, therefore, must be exercised to see that the visuals and the commentary are well synchronized, especially in teaching oriented programmes. A few students (again from Bangalore) have also suggested that minute and internal parts of dissected flowers should be magnified and focussed upon, by the camera so that students sitting in a classroom viewing situation can see better.

Students from majority of the locations have also pointed out that the pace of narration or commentary was very fast. Care must be taken to maintain an optimum speed. This is particularly important because it is a programme giving high amount of factual information and secondly, the viewers consist of a heterogeneous group of both students who are familiar and those who are unfamiliar with the concept.

Prashna or Question

Reports from all the locations have indicated that a very small sample sat through and viewed this programme. The two reasons stated by them for this were first, fatigue had set in and two, the superimposition of two languages and both unknown in most places, led to boredom and frustration.

The report from Pune also states that in spite of Marathi being a local language the programme was not understood. An interesting observation made here was that the dubbing in English went alongside the original Marathi dialogue at the same speed and volume. This tended to create confusion. While some mentioned that they found the programme neither educative nor entertaining, many commented that the theme was good, serious and relevant but the unclear language hindered their comprehension. In Ahmedabad a very small number of students indicated that they understood something of the programme, and this group also mainly consisted of urban English medium students.

Indian Programmes—A Comparison

Although we have mentioned earlier that programmes on general issues seem to interest a large audience, two of the three Indian programmes, namely 'Introduction of Computers' and 'Flowers', though specific in nature, were appreciated better than the third 'Prashna' meant to be general in nature.

'Introduction to Computers' has been rated as most interesting by students of Ahmedabad and Pune, while Gorakhpur students find 'Flower'—

most interesting. There was a split in the reactions of the Hyderabad students. The urban students found 'Introduction to Computers' most interesting, while rural students 'Flower'. The reason for this could be the difference in the amount of previous exposure, or familiarity with the topic.

With regard to vocabulary 'Introduction to Computers' was rated high. This programme was also found to be the most inspiring and providing valuable information compared to the other two. Regarding the second and third preference, data indicates that 'Flower' always got the second preference, while 'Prashna' hardly got mentioned. Actually, on the whole, a very small percentage of students watched 'Prashna' completely. The reasons mentioned were lack of comprehension of the language (due to the superimposition of two languages), electricity failure in a few places and also being the last of the programmes to be pre-tested, fatigue had crept in and students were not very keen on viewing the entire programme.

EXPERIENCES FROM PRE-TESTING

After having undertaken such a nation wide pre-testing one can point out the limitations and learning experiences. Also with regard to methodology one can state a few dos and dont's which one ought to take care of the next time such a project is to be conducted. One common comment made by students, teachers, project leaders and observers is that the pre-testing sessions should not be of very long duration. The length of each individual programme should be around 15 to 20 minutes so that the total time taken for each pre-testing, that is inclusive of administering the questionnaire would not exceed 35 to 40 minutes. Also the number of programmes to be pre-tested in each session should not exceed two. One says two, because students find it difficult to hold their attention for more than 30 to 40 minutes at a time. Boredom and frustration sets in and this has detrimental effects on the absorption power and performance of the student.

The second important feature is with regard to the pre-testing questionnaire. Long descriptive questions should be avoided as it requires the student to spend a lot more time on answering it. Question in the multiple choice format seem to be much more effective in terms of administering, as it becomes easier for the student as well the researcher. The wording too, should be precise and as simple as possible, so as to aid those students who have a minimum knowledge of English.

Suggestions related to Programme Technique

The results of the pre-testing also throws light on some of the production techniques which might help in producing better educational programmes in future. These are based on the observation and comments made by the students and the researchers :

(a) Length of the programmes should not exceed 20-22 minutes,
(b) A facilitator (Indian) does help, in the sense, it helps in conditioning the audience to the content of the programme,
(c) Facilitator if being presented in the end, should be introduced before the programme credits appear as otherwise the facilitator goes unheard,
(d) Summaries, written and verbal are a great help,
(e) Summaries or intervention in regional language would be of great help to enhance comprehension,
(f) Technical names like Latin botanical names should be supplemented with local coloquially used terminology so as to aid identification and retention,
(g) Audio recording should be as clear as possible so that even non-English speaking students can try and follow,
(h) The pace of the commentary should be slower. That is, the number of words per minute should be reduced to help comprehension,
(i) Care should be taken to synchronize the visuals and commentary properly,
(j) Close ups of details and internal minute parts should be shown so that a large group in a class room viewing situation are able to see clearly,
(k) The documentary format is appreciated more than the lecture type method,
(l) Demonstration technique is appreciated but seems effective only when presenting simple scientific concepts,
(m) Dubbing in two languages, or superimposition of English on a regional language at the same speed and volume, should be avoided as it is a total failure. Preferably commentary should be in one language only,
(n) Programmes related to current issues like the energy crisis are much more appreciated compared to programmes on specific concepts,
(o) Effective music with the commentary goes a long way in holding the attention of the viewers, and
(p) Films in colour had higher attention holding capacity as they were more appealing.

The foregoing analyses and some of the production recommendations are based on the limited experience of pre-testing six programmes in five locations. It is necessary that periodic pre-testing of selected programmes must continue to provide inputs for programme production. Such pre-testings should be systematically done to cover areas which are not covered by the present study. In general, it would be most desirable to conduct a pre-testing before initiating new programmes by any of the centres. Also equally important would be to initiate script testing in some of the selected areas before starting actual production.

5

MESSAGE SYSTEM ANALYSIS OF UGC COUNTRYWIDE CLASSROOM

BINOD C. AGRAWAL, JAWAID NEZAM HASHMI, IMTIAZ KAR, ARBIND K. SINHA AND JYOTSNA VERMA

INTRODUCTION

SHORTLY, "INSAT Countrywide Classroom" is completing its fourth year of operation. In the last four years, it has transmitted over 1500 hours of educational programmes for the undergraduate students studying in 5000 colleges dotted over the country-metropolitan cities, small towns and in rural setting. As the same programme capsule is repeated twice a day, the original transmission is half the total telecast hours. As the production tempo has accelerated over the period due to expansion of production facilities the dependency for the programmes on the international agencies has reduced. While production capabilities have improved, the related communication research has not found similar enthusiasm in the total strategy of using television for high quality university level education. The first communication research effort however, was made in early 1984 to pre-test some of the television programmes to evaluate their usefulness for transmission. Since then, many efforts have been made to understand the nature and characteristics of viewers. Some pre-production research is also underway, including an utilization study of UGC programmes by college students. In this study our aim is three-fold :

(a) To evolve a method of message system analysis for country-wide classroom,
(b) To analyse one month's country-wide classroom message system in the light of UGC countrywide classroom philosophy and approach, and
(c) Present, if any, broad recommendations and implications emerging from the message system analysis.

The State of Art

The message system analysis as an important research technique in the field of Social Science is fairly old. It has had wide applicability in a large number of academics disciplines. Barcus (1969 : 539-554) reported wide range teaching and applications of content analysis techniques in the North American universities. Among other disciplines of social sciences and humanities, education was also found using message system analysis extensively (Barcus, 1969 : 539-554). The first major summary of researches related to content analysis was published by Berelson (1952) who has earlier jointly published a book on this topic (Berelson and Lazarsfeld, 1948).[1]

Trends in Content Analysis (Pool, 1959) attracted the attention of social scientists in several disciplines. This book was a result of the first conference on content analysis held in the United States of America during 1955. Similar efforts have been made in other parts of the world, in which European scholars have had given lead and showed great interest in the content analysis (Krippendorff, 1980 : 13-20). The most popular use of this technique relates to content analysis of political messages. Publications authored by North *et al.* (1963), Stone *et al.* (1966) and Gerbner *et al.* (1969) apart from others were significant contributions in improving the method of content analysis during sixties. These publications helped in defining the scope and refining the methodology of the content analysis. By then the concept of "message system analysis" was advocated by Gerbner (1969). Gerbner (1969 : 123) felt that "The systematic analysis of message content is a traditional area of study in communication research and related fields. ...But none of the new frameworks and approaches presented considers the analysis of message systems addressed to heterogeneous and anonymous public, such as mass communications,..." (Gerbner, 1969 : 123). The present countrywide classroom television programmes fall in the public domain. Hence, it should be analysed as a message system and the same has been followed in this study.

In seventies computer approach was increasingly followed for message system analysis (Krippendorff 1980). In the global perspective "Currently, content analysis is somewhat at a crossroad. Its history is

1. "Content Analysis is a research technique for making applicable and valid inferences from data to their context". (Krippendorff 1980 : 21). Further it provides..."objective, systematic and quantitative description of the manifest content of communication" Berelson (1952 : 18 quoted by Krippendorff 1980 : 21).

rooted in the journalistic fascination with numbers, supposedly making a quantitative statement more convincing than a qualitative one. Content analysis could continue the counting game which may lead to excitement but not to insights. Content analysis could also pursue more seriously than it has in the past what is involved in the claim to analyse something that is recognizably symbolic as a symbolic phenomenon, tracing its social role, effects, and meaning" (Krippendorff 1980 : 7). The present effort of the message system analysis is in the above perspective. Within India, message system analysis of television programmes are not many. In agriculture extension some efforts were made to content analyse, the agricultural message of **Krishi Darshan** and other development programmes (Chauhan, 1980). Some similar efforts within Doordarshan were also made on small scale but none of these studies have been published. During Satellite Instructional Television Experiment (SITE) an earnest effort was made to establish a "Message System Analysis" group. Several coding instruments for message system analysis of SITE programmes in a comparative perspective were developed (See Mody and Sarupria; 1976, Mody; 1977 and 1979).

Following a similar method several attempts have been made to content analyse the programme of Kheda Communication Project (Joshi, Shah and Misra; 1984, Misra; 1984 and 1985, Brace; 1984, Shah; 1984). In some schools of Journalism and Communication in which lead has been provided by Osmania University few theses on content analysis have also been attempted. But majority of them relates to print medium and a very few to radio and television (Prasad, 1986). In the recent past, some efforts have been made to content analyse countrywide classroom programmes (See Ila Joshi, 1987). Keeping in view that the "Countrywide Classroom" project is intended to broaden the horizon of the college students, provide latest information and add to their existing knowledge, using empirical approach, the effort made here is to evolve a method by which one can project and predict the expected effects of TV programmes on the viewers.

In the Indian context, it is very important as the messages are meant for a multi-cultural and multi-linguistic students who are expected to share common communication in English language that too emanating from various cultural and linguistic settings of the world. This makes it difficult to share "common meanings". Further, in such a situation, there cannot be a single meaning of the message even though some of them are considered to be "universal" and accepted by a large majority as "scientific truth". Keeping this in view the attempt here is to provide "designations analysis" which "provides the frequency with which certain objects (persons, things, groups and concepts) are referred to that is roughly speaking subject—matter analysis" (Krippendorff, 1980 : 33). It is an exploratory study to evolve an appropriate method for higher education television message system analysis, especially where there is little evidence of the message system analysis technique being utilized for the educational television especially for higher education. Given the discipline based nature and scope of the programmes, such an analysis might not have been favoured by the communication researchers, academics and subject matter specialist alike in other parts of the world. But in our situation, it will yield results for improving and better utilization of the television for higher education.

Evolving Research Tools for Message System Analysis

In the absence of any readymade research tool for the message system analysis our first task was to evolve a research design and an appropriate tool for this study. Our first step was to define the research design in such a way that we could do meaningful analysis of the educational programmes within the socio-cultural context to make it "context sensitive" research design. This meant that there must be an explicit correspondence between the method followed for the study and the Credo defined by the University Grants Commission. This would then provide a base for the message system analysis of the UGC Countrywide Classroom. The basic aim of the UGC Countrywide Classroom is defined "to up date, to up grade and enrich the quality of education, while extending its reach". The programmes are expected to "arouse the interest of the viewers, to whet their appetite and broaden their horizons. The aim is to stimulate and not to satiate". Keeping this kind of objective in view we looked for a research design and that too a "sequential" one as we wanted to examine the content of the programme both as a unit and then broken into parts on per minute basis.

As a first step, we collected all the studies conducted here and elsewhere which indicated the paucity of relevant research for present purpose. Therefore, we followed a text book approach, combined two research designs namely, (1) the design to estimate, and (2) the design to test the suitability of the programme. The estimate design was utilized to analyse the programme composition of Indian and Foreign origin; expected transmission hours and actual transmission duration; time distribution for various disciplines and on the presentation of new findings. The second design was implied to test the differences in both quantity and quality of Indian and Foreign programmes, thereby testing the suitability of these programmes for the target audiences. (for details see Krippendorff, 1980 : 49-55).

As an urgency was expressed by the sponsers of the research, it was felt that about 30 hours of original transmission would yield approximately 70 to 80 programmes for message system analysis. Accordingly, the month of February-March were selected for this purpose (February 2 to March 2, 1988). After a careful analysis of the weekly transmission schedule, it was clear that a logic was being followed in the transmission schedule, which was consistent, over a period of time. Therefore, four weeks transmission provided a good sample of what is being transmitted under the UGC Countrywide Classroom programmes. Thus, the sample for the present analysis consists of a total of 62 programmes. Table 5.1 provides the distribution of the programmes by production agencies. Sample has broad presentation of agencies.

Table 5.1 : Distribution of the Programmes by Production Agencies

Sr. No.	*Production Agency (Indian)*	*No. of Prog-rammes*	*Duration in Minutes*	*Production Agency (Foreign)*	*No. of Prog-rammes*	*Duration in Minutes*
1.	MCRC, Delhi	6	130	UK	1	9
2.	EMRC, Ahmedabad	7	131	USSR	2	46
3.	EMRC, Hyderabad	7	145	USA	5	131
4.	EMRC, Pune	9	159	Canada	1	23
5.	AVRC, Roorkee	2	59	FRG	3	69
6.	AVRC, Hyderabad	2	39	Australia	3	95
7.	AVRC, Madras	3	56			
8.	AVRC, Jodhpur	1	18			
9.	AVRC, Calcutta	4	75			
10.	TTTI, Bhopal	2	37			
11.	PTI, New Delhi	1	19			
12.	DECU, Ahmedabad	2	43			
13.	Others	1	26			
	Total	47	937		15	373

Note : One programme was jointly produced by MCRC, Delhi and AVRC, Madurai

The most critical aspect of the effort was to evolve instruments for data coding/unitizing the programmes. The observation sheet for coding various components of a programme was developed. Keeping in view the objectives of the UGC programmes and the possible methods for direct observation in laboratory situations, a preliminary instrument was evolved. The same was discussed with the research staff of the Educational Media Research Centre, Ahmedabad who had conducted a content analysis study earlier. The same was also discussed with Professor E.V. Chitnis who brought out some of the dimensions that could be examined through message system analysis. Thus, a preliminary message system analysis instrument was evolved and was tested by five researchers who sat in front of television and tried to fill the observation sheet after viewing the programmes. Immediately we found several difficulties in filling the observation sheet. So a process of revision began in which the sequence of the questions were modified several times. Efforts were made to convert open-ended-questions of close-ended-questions. Also a number of questions were dropped. This process took more than a week of continuous viewing of UGC programmes both in the morning and in the evening. At this stage, it was equally important to design observation sheet in such a way that it could be amenable to quick computer analysis. Also the project leader wanted to have built in some redundant questions which would help in checking the internal validity and consistency of the observation sheet.

Parallel to the above activity was to evolve another observation sheet in which six production components on minute to minute basis could be analysed along with the educational elements of each programme. Basically, this instrument was to gauge the differences that might exist between Indian and Foreign programmes and the pedagogic approach followed in these programmes for education if any. The most important difficulty was the operationalization of each component so that the observers could code the observation sheet with minimal disagreement. In consultation with television producers especially Mr. K. Vishwanath of ISRO, Ahmedabad and after several trial tests various components were evolved. Thus, with this process we were able to evolve two instruments known as Message System Analysis 01 and Message System Analysis 02. (See Appendices 1 and 2).

Having limited manpower the research team who was responsible for evolving the instruments went through rigorous training to act as coders. Training for this purpose was given after repeated viewing of few programmes. A continuous discussion among the coders took place, who clarified each others' doubts and reached to certain consensus on the coding method. This method of training helped to reduce individual disagreements on various aspects of coding.

While the instruments were being finalized video tapes for the actual programmes transmitted from February 2, 1988 onwards were taped on 1/2" VHS every day until March 2, 1988.

The actual method followed in television programme coding involved three stages. In the first stage a total of five coders, (at least three at any time) viewed the programme and filled the Message System Analysis 01 observation sheet. In the second stage, the same method was repeated in which Message System Analysis 02 was coded.

In the third stage, these coders brought together their coded sheets and prepared a common observation sheet. If there were any disagreements about a particular code, it was discussed and an agreed code was given. Sometimes, if it was not resolved the coders had to re-run the programme to reach to a common code. When the agreement was high the common observation sheet was prepared just by looking at other observation sheets. On an average three hours were required to complete the coding of an hour programme.

From February 17 to March 2, 1988 live programmes were viewed and coded twice a day as per the schedule. But the data from February 2 to 16 were viewed after March 2, 1988. This has provided the total data for analysis. The list of the programmes produced are in Appendix 2.

Method of Analysis

As indicated earlier, both observation sheets were designed in such a way that the data could be directly transferred to computer on dBase. Accordingly all data were transferred to dBase and after the first run, all checkings were done. Clean data were run for tabulation in which the Indian and Foreign programmes were separately analysed. To start with, frequency analysis of all the elements of all questions were done. Based on the frequency distribution analysis further selected analysis were conducted. Correlations between selected elements were also attempted.

The Analysis of Message System

During February 2 to March 2, 1988 it was expected that there would be twenty-six days of telecast. On each day there would be two telecasts of one hour each. Table 5.2 shows that out of a total 52 expected hours of telecast, the programmes were transmitted for 41 hours only. In other words, about one-fifth or 21.2 per cent of the time was not utilized. Equally significant is that there were no prior announcements regarding cancellation of the telecast. All efforts should be made to reduce the cancellations and if unavoidable alternate timings should be provided and appropriate announcements should be made. Further analysis shows that the countrywide classroom programme was telecast for 218 hours or 1310 minutes out of 24 hours or 1440 minutes transmission. Table 5.3 shows that 9 per cent of transmission was used for various purposes in which the most significant was 14 'fillers' in 24 days of telecast. These fillers were confusing as they were 'packaged' along with the main programmes and in most cases, on the related topics. There are two suggestions for better utilization of the 'fillers'. One, strict discipline should be followed in deciding the duration of both single and serial programmes. Second all efforts should be made to produce flexible short duration fillers on 'general knowledge', 'Do you know', 'Physical laws' and 'New discoveries'. These should be packaged instead of the present method.

Out of sixty-two programmes of 1310 minutes duration telecast, 47 or 75.8 per cent were produced by various Educational Media Research Centres, Audio Visual Research Centres and other Indian production agencies. The remaining 15 or 24.2 per cent programmes were produced by six foreign countries (See Table 5.1 for full details). It shows reduction in the foreign programmes from the initial years of the countrywide classroom. Majority of the 15 foreign programmes telecast are on science subjects that too in the areas of emerging disciplines.

Table 5.2 : Utilization of Telecast Time between February 2 to March 2, 1988

Utilization Pattern	*Scheduled Telecast Hours*		*Total*
	12.45 to 13.45	*1600 to 1700*	
Actual Utilization in Hours	23 (88.5)	18 (69.2)	41 (78.8)
Non-Utilization in Hours	3 (11.5)	8 (30.8)	11 (21.2)
Expected Utilization in Hours	26 (100)	26 (100)	52 (100)

Note : The figures in parenthesis are percentages.

An attempt was made to understand the programme duration of the programmes. Table 5.4 provides the distribution of the programmes according to time duration. On an average a programme was about 21.1 minutes long regardless of the production origin. While largest number (23) of Indian programmes were of 16 to 20 minutes duration, the Foreign programmes (10) were of 21 to 25 minutes. Given the time limitation it would be desirable to have more programmes of shorter duration especially of the foreign origin.

Table 5.3 : Percentage Distribution of Estimated Transmission Time Utilization between February 2 to March 2, 1988

Sr. No.	*Utilization Purpose*	*Duration in Minutes*	*Percentage*
1.	Doordarshan Signature Tune	24	1.7
2.	UGC Caption	10	0.7
3.	Today's and Tomorrow's Programme Announcement	36	2.5
4.	Next Week's Programme Announcements	9	0.6
5.	Countrywide Classroom Programmes	1310	91.0
6.	Fillers	43	3.0
7.	Request for Feedback	8	0.5
	Total	1440	100

Note : The calculation includes 23 hours of 12.45 to 13.45 hours telecast and one hour of 16.00 to 17.00 hours telecast. The remaining hours out of 41 hours were telecast from 16.00 to 17.00 hours of the noon programme.

All the sixty-two programmes (both of Indian and Foreign origin) were colour productions. These programmes were divided into two categories. The first category consisted of "Single Slot" programmes defined as an independent programme on a single topic or concept. The second category referred to as a "series" in which several programmes on a broad educational discipline or topic was produced as serial.

Table 5.4 : Percentage Distribution of Programme Duration by Indian and Foreign Production

Sr. No.	*Duration in Minutes*	*Indian*	*Foreign*	*Total*
1.	Less than 10 minutes	6.4	6.7	6.5
		(3)	(1)	(4)
2.	Between 11 to 15 minutes	6.4	13.3	8.1
		(3)	(2)	(5)
3.	Between 16 to 20 minutes	48.9	6.7	38.7
		(23)	(1)	(24)
4.	Between 21 to 30 minutes	36.2	66.6	43.5
		(17)	(10)	(27)
5.	Between 31 to 35 minutes	2.1	6.7	3.2
		(1)	(1)	(2)
	Total	100	100	100
		(47)	(15)	(62)

Note : Figures in parenthesis are frequencies.

Table 5.5 shows that there were more "series" in the foreign programmes when compared with Indian programmes. It may be due to multiple agencies involvement in the production within the country or due to variety of topics that ought to be covered. Another explanation (based the analysis of the topics covered) could be that initial production fascination might have lead to selection of topics without a focus. Policy decision will help in determining the production direction to achieve desired goal.

Table 5.5 : Percentage Distribution of "Single Slot" and "Series" Programmes by Indian and Foreign Origin

Sr. No.	*Programme Type*	*Indian*	*Foreign*	*Total*
1.	Single Slot	68.1	53.3	64.5
		(32)	(8)	(40)
2.	Series	31.9	46.7	35.5
		(15)	(7)	(22)
3.	Total	47.0	15.0	62.0
		(75.8)	(24.2)	(100)

Note : Figures in the parenthesis are frequencies.

Programme Presentation Loci

Distinct differences have been observed between Indian and Foreign programmes in terms of their production grammer. While 40.4 per cent of the Indian programmes were shot within studio/indoors, 73.3 per cent foreign programmes were shot outdoors/related field locations. Similarly, 23.4 per cent Indian programmes were shot within a laboratory/scientific setting as compared to 6.7 per cent of the Foreign programmes. The interesting difference observed is the "lecture format" that continues to dominate the Indian educational production whereas majority of the Foreign programmes seemed to be "general purpose" and "informational" programmes. (See Table 5.6).

Collaborated by the results of Tables 5.7 and 5.8. Table 5.7 shows that the objectives of 68.1 per cent or 32 individual Indian programmes were defined. Whereas it was 60 per cent in the case of Foreign programmes (See Table 5.7). Further 46.8 per cent Indian programmes are appropriate for the students of Science, Arts and Commerce. The corresponding figures for the Foreign programmes are 66.7 per cent (See Table 5.8). The disturbing observation in the Table 5.8 is that 19.2 per cent or 9 Indian programmes have been judged as "inappropriate" for under-graduate

Table 5.6 : Percentage Distribution of Production Loci between Indian and Foreign Programmes

Sr. No.	*Production Loci*	*Indian*	*Foreign*	*Total*
1.	Home/Indoor/Studio Office Chamber	40.4 (19)	6.7 (1)	32.32 (20)
2.	Class/Seminar Conference room/Hall	8.5 (4)	13.3 (2)	9.7 (6)
3.	Laboratory/Factory Industrial/Scientific Setting	23.4 (11)	6.7 (1)	19.4 (12)
4.	Related field location/ Natural Surrounding/ outdoor	27.7 (13)	73.3 (12)	38.7 (24)
	Total	100 (47)	100 (15)	100 (62)

Note : Figures in the parenthesis are frequencies.

students of any of the three faculties. What emerged from the analysis is that a large majority of Foreign programmes are 'informational' meant for general audience. Therefore, future selection of such programmes should be done in the light of present philosophy and approach of the UGC countrywide classroom. Also there is a need for careful evaluation of the Indian programmes regarding their appropriateness for the target audience.

Programme Content and UGC Credo

The UGC programme "Credo" for countrywide classroom was formulated almost three years after it actually started in 1984 and Audio Visual Research Centres prior to 1987. Forty seven Indian programmes telecast during February 2 to March 2, 1988 had a number of programmes

Table 5.7 : Percentage Distribution of the Defined Objectives of the Programmes by Indian and Foreign Production

Sr. No.	*Objectives*	*Indian*	*Foreign*	*Total*
1.	Defined	68.1 (32)	60.0 (9)	66.1 (41)
2.	Not Defined	31.9 (15)	40.0 (6)	33.9 (21)
	Total	100 (47)	100 (15)	100 (62)

Note : Figures in the parenthesis are frequencies.

Table 5.8 : Percentage Distribution of the Programme Appropriateness by Indian and Foreign Production

Sr. No.	*Appropriate*	*Indian*	*Foreign*	*Total*
1.	For Science Students	25.5 (12)	33.3 (5)	27.4 (17)
2.	For Arts Students	8.5 (4)	–	6.5 (4)
3.	For All Students	46.8 (22)	66.7 (10)	51.6 (32)
4.	For none of the students	19.2 (9)	–	14.5 (9)
	Total	100 (47)	100 (15)	100 (62)

Note : There was no programme for Commerce Students.
Figure in parenthesis are frequencies.

produced earlier. But one cannot lose sight that even in the initial documents the UGC credo was in germane in its nascent form. In the present study, one of the areas investigated was to test the extent to which the programme confirmed with "The UGC Countrywide Classroom philosophy and approach". Another related area was to find out whether the programmes had any gender bias. The qualitative judgements showed that all the sixty two programmes were "gender neutral". Further qualitative analysis will be required to substantiate this qualitative finding which is being attempted.

Table 5.9 : Percentage Distribution of the Motivating Abilities of the Programmes by Indian and Foreign Production

Sr. No.	*Ability to Motivate*	*Indian*	*Foreign*	*Total*
1.	Did Motivate	29.8 (14)	26.7 (4)	29.0 (18)
2.	Did not motivate	70.2 (33)	73.3 (11)	71.0 (44)
	Total	100 (47)	100 (15)	100 (62)

Note : Figure in parethesis are frequencies.

Table 5.9 shows with Indian and Foreign programmes had uniformally low ability to motivate the viewers (in this case students) to do something or think about the programme. Serious efforts would be required to produce programme which can motivate students to do or think some new ideas. A similar pattern can be observed in Table 5.10. Wherein both

Indian and Foreign programmes seemed to lack in their efforts to inculcate scientific/rational attitude or temper to solve problems. This lack may be due to subject matter of the programmes. However, regardless of the programme content one can create an attitude of enquiry, rational and scientific attitude towards solving problems which should be attempted in the future programme especially those produced within India.

Table 5.10 : Percentage Distribution of Inculcating Scientific Attitude by Indian and Foreign Programmes

Sr. No.	*Scientific Attitude*	*Indian*	*Foreign*	*Total*
1.	Attempted to inculcate Scientific attitude	19.2 (9)	13.3 (3)	-19.4 (12)
2.	Did not attempt to inculcate sci-entific attitude	80.8 (38)	86.7 (22)	80.6 (50)
	Total	100 (47)	100 (15)	100 (62)

Note : Figures in parenthesis are frequencies.

Another dimension examined of whether the programme helped to open up new areas of understanding related to 'new developments', 'discoveries', 'approaches' and 'new emerging trends'.

Table 5.11 : Percentage Distribution of Programmes which Helped New Areas of Understanding by Indian and Foreign Production

Sr. No.	*Programme helped New Areas of Understanding*	*Indian*	*Foreign*	*Total*
1.	No	70.0 (33)	80.0 (12)	72.6 (45)
2.	Yes	29.8 (14)	20.0 (3)	27.4 (17)
	Total	100 (47)	100 (15)	100 (62)

Note : Figures in parenthesis are frequencies.

Table 5.11 shows that 29.8 per cent Indian and 20 per cent of Foreign programmes seemed to be helpful, in opening up new areas of understanding. In the traditional educational process, the transfer of knowledge and skill are important aspects of teaching and learning. An input of more than one quarter of the programmes devoted to new areas of understanding is a positive sign towards achieving UGC Credo. However, one is tempted to say that an over arching consideration in all these programmes should be updating and upgrading of knowledge thereby helping the students to enrich their understanding. This could be attempted by integrating new information in the existing text book knowledge. This is especially true for Social Science programmes.

On the whole, social/physical sciences programmes were presented in an universal perspective while programmes related to 'development' and 'Art' were within the context of India and dealt with local issues. Table 5.12 provides detailed percentage distribution of the programmes in which the concepts were contextualized/localized or universalized. Table 5.12 shows that 58.0 programmes were universalized on both cases. In case of the Indian programmes the contextualized and localized programmes dealt with national issues and programmes.

Table 5.12 : Percentage Distribution of Programmes According to Level of Programme Universalization by Indian and Foreign Production

Sr. No.	*Level of Universalization*	*Indian*	*Foreign*	*Total*
1.	Programme contextua-lized	23.4 (11)	6.7 (1)	19.4 (12)
2.	Programme localized	19.2 (9)	33.3 (5)	22.6 (14)
3.	Programme Univer-salized	57.4 (27)	60.0 (9)	58.0 (36)
	Total	100 (47)	100 (15)	100 (62)

Note : The figures in parenthesis are frequencies.

The next two questions asked whether the programmes raised ideas for questioning/pondering over important national issues like unemployment, population, pollution and emerging crisis and whether programmes conveyed broader/bigger purposes of life. On both accounts it was observed that a very few programmes raised these issues. (See Tables 5.13 and 5.14).

Table 5.13 : Percentage Distribution of the Programmes Raising Broader Issues by Indian and Foreign Programmes

Sr. No.	*Broader Issues*	*Indian*	*Foreign*	*Total*
1.	Raised	14.9 (7)	13.3 (2)	14.5 (9)
2.	Not Raised	63.8 (30)	80.0 (12)	67.7 (42)
3.	Not Possible to raise	21.3 (10)	6.7 (1)	17.7 (11)
	Total	100 (47)	100 (15)	100 (62)

Note : The figures in parenthesis are frequencies.

Table 5.14 : Percentage Distribution of the programmes Raising Bigger Purpose of Life by Indian and Foreign Programme.

Sr. No.	*Bigger purpose of life*	*Indian*	*Foreign*	*Total*
1.	Raised	4.3	13.3	6.5
		(2)	(2)	(4)
2.	Not Raised	63.8	80.0	67.7
		(30)	(12)	(42)
3.	Not Possible to Raise	31.9	6.7	25.8
		(15)	(1)	(16)
	Total	100	100	100
		(47)	(15)	(62)

Note : The figures in Parenthesis are frequencies.

Programme Production and Educational Content Quality

Efforts to gauge the production and educational quality of the programmes were attempted. For this purpose two simple "summated scales" were evolved. Items related to visual, sound, colour, pronunciation, pace, tone, audio and graphics were utilized for evaluating the "production quality". Similarly, nine items were utilized to evaluate the educational content quality of the programmes, Tables 5.15 and 5.16 provide analysis on both issues.

Table 5.15 shows that none of the foreign programmes were considered "good" whereas 80.9 per cent of the Indian programmes were considered fair. The remaining 19.1 per cent Indian programmes were considered good. Keeping in view the production quality there is need for the improvement in the production quality.

Table 5.16 shows that for not more than 21 per cent of the programmes could quality to be called "good" in terms of their educational content. But more than 30 per cent of them were rated poor. There is a need to improve the educational content of the programmes both of the Indian and Foreign origin. The analysis of Tables 5.15 and 5.16 suggest that there is need for overall improvement in the production quality if one expects to have positive impact of these programmes on the undergraduate students of widely scattered colleges in the country.

Educational content quality is based on the variables like : programmes which specify objective, motivate viewer, not containing too many technical terms, circulate rational attitude, open up new area of understanding, message universalized, raised broad issues, convey bigger purpose of life and recapitulate main ideas.

Table 5.15 : Production Quality of Programmes by Indian and Foreign Production

Sr. No.	*Production Quality*	*Indian*	*Foreign*	*Total*
1.	Good	19.0	–	14.5
		(9)	0	(9)
2.	Fair	81.0	100	85.5
		(38)	(15)	(53)
3.	Poor	–	–	–
	Total	100	100	100
		(47)	(15)	(62)

Note : Eight variables were used in determining the production quality of the programme. These are :

Visual	Pace
Sound	Tone
Colour	Audio, and
Pronunciation	Graphics

Table 5.16 : Percentage Distribution of Educational Content Quality by Indian and Foreign Production

Sr. No.	*Content Quality*	*Indian*	*Foriegn*	*Total*
1.	Good	21.2	20.0	21.0
		(10)	(3)	(13)
2.	Fair	46.8	47.0	47.0
		(22)	(7)	(29)
3.	Poor	32.0	33.0	32.0
		(15)	(5)	(20)
	Total	100	100	100
		(47)	(15)	(62)

Concluding Comments

This study aimed at evolving a method of message system analysis for country-wide classroom; present, if any, broad recommendations and implications emerging from the study.

Review of literature indicated paucity of relevant research for present purpose. Therefore, a textbook approach was followed. This combined two research designs namely, (1) the design to estimate (Message Content) and (2) design to test the suitability of the programme for undergraduate student. Several rounds of discussions, consultation and trial tests, the instruments were evolved. Observation sheets were designed in such a way that the data was directly transferred to computer on dBase. One month data were coded for this study by a panel of coders. Data were analysed for Indian and Foreign programmes separately.

* All efforts should be made to reduce the cancellations and it unavoidable alternate timings should be provided and appropriate announcements should be made.
* Better utilization of the "fillers" : strict discipline should be followed in deciding the duration of both "single" and "serial" programmes. And all efforts should be made to produce flexible short duration fillers on "general knowledge".
* Given the time limitation, it would be desirable to have more programmes of shorter duration especially if they are of the Foreign origin.
* A large majority of Foreign programmes are "informational" meant for general audience. Therefore, future selection of such programmes should be done in the light of present philosophy and approach of the UGC countrywide classroom. Also there is need for careful evaluation of the Indian programmes regarding their appropriateness for the target audience.
* Serious efforts would be required to produce programme which can motivate students to do or think about some new ideas.
* Programmes efforts should be such that it can create an attitude of enquiry, rational and scientific attitude towards solving problems especially those produced within the country.
* There is a room to improve the production quality as well as educational content of the programmes. Same should be attempted with the help of content matter specialists and communication researchers.

APPENDIX I

MSA 01

DEVELOPMENT AND EDUCATIONAL COMMUNICATION UNIT AHMEDABAD

Message System Analysis of INSAT Countrywide Class Room

1. Coder's name :
2. Date : Day :
3. Programme no : 1 2 3 4 (Filler)
4. Transmission time : a. 12.45 to 1.45 b. 4.00 to 5.00
5. Title of the programme :
6. Duration of programme : Minutes......... Seconds..........
7. Was the programme : 1 Black and white...... 2 Colour.........
8. Was the programme : 1 Single slot........... 2 Series.........
9. Production Agency :

Indian

1. EMRC/MCRC : 1. Delhi, 2. Ahmebadad, 3. Hyderabad, 4. Poona
2. AVRC : 1. Roorkee, 2. Hybad, 3. Madras, 4. Jodhpur, 5. Calcutta 6. Madurai
3. Others : 1. TTTI, 2. PTI, 3. DECU, 4. Other (write) :

Foreign

1. UK, 2. USSR, 3. USA, 4. Canada, 5. FRG, 6. Australia, 7. Other (write) :

11. Code for quality of transmission :
    1. Visual—1. Excellent, 2. Good, 3. Fair, 4. Poor
    2. Sound—1. Excellent, 2. Good, 3. Fair, 4. Poor
    3. Colour—1. Uniformaly good, 2. Good, 3. Fluctuations, BW/C, 4. Bad

12. Indicate loci of activity/presentation/show
    1. Home/indoor/office
    2. Classroom/seminar/conference room/hall
    3. Laboratory/factory/industrial/scientific setting
    4. Related field location/natural surrounding

13. Indicate human participation in the programme and their approximate number by gender

	Male	*Female*	*Total*
1. Expert/lecturer			
2. Student/learner			
3. Anchorperson/compere			
4. Others			

14. Indicate pronunciation/Pace and tone of audio by expert/lecturer/presenter/commentator/compere :

* Pronunciation	:	1. Excellent	2. Good	3. Poor
* Pace	:	1. Slow	2. Medium	3. Fast
* Tone	:	1. Humourous	2. Monotonous	3. Serious
* Audio	:	1. Audible	2. Feeble	3. Inaudible

15. Indicate the quality of the following in the programme

	1 Excellent	*2 Good*	*3 Poor*	*4 Not used*
1. Graphics				
2. Chart/Graph				
3. Table				
4. Caption				
5. Still picture				
6. Animation				

16. Were there any spelling errors in the written text of the programme?
    1. Yes, 2. No, 3. Not applicable
17. Were there any grammatical error in the programme spoken or written? 1. Yes, 2. No, 3. Not applicable
18. Whether the objective/s of the programmes was/were clearly specified? 1. Yes, 2. No, 3. Not applicable
19. Was the content of the programme appropriate for undergraduate students of 1. science 2. commerce 3. arts 4. all of these 5. None of these
20. Did the programme motivate the viewer to do something or think about the programme? 1. Yes 2. No
21. Did the programme contain too many technical/scientific terms, figures, numbers and statistics which might hamper understanding and recall? 1. Yes 2. No
22. Did the programme attempt to inculcate : scientific/rational attitude/temper to solve problems
    1. Yes 2. No 3. Not applicable
23. Did the programme deal with elementary/advance/difficult concepts for undergraduate students?
    1. Yes 2. No 3. Not applicable
24. Whether the programme helped to open up new areas of understanding? 1. Yes 2. No

If yes, did it contain 1. New developments, 2. Discoveries, 3. Approaches, 4. New emerging trends

25. Was the programme concept/message
    1. contextualized, 2. localized, 3. universalized?
26. Whether broader issues for questioning/pondering over unemployment, population, pollution, energy crisis etc. were raised?
    1. Yes 2. No 3. Not applicable
27. Did the programme convey broader/bigger purpose of life?
    1. Yes 2. No 3. Not applicable
28. What educational pedagogy was followed in the programme?
    1. Skill transfer 2. Interactive 3. Question raising
29. Whether the main ideas/process were recapitulated in the programme?
    1. Yes 2. No
    If yes, how many times
30. Was this programme
    1. gender neutral 2. pro-male 3. pro-female?
31. Was there a distinct feeling that the programme was a
    1. Demonstration (real and Simulated)
    2. Lecture/Expert speaking/illustrated lecture
    3. Panel Discussion/Interview/Press conference/Talk/show/Quiz
    4. Documentary/(Narrative, Simulated, Actual)
    5. Drama (with real actors/puppets/animation/story)
    6. Cultural/Musical performance
32. Mention the broader discipline the programme covers
    ....
33. Producer : 1. NM 2. Mentioned
34. Script Writer : 1. NM 2. Mentioned
35. Subject Expert : 1. NM 2. Mentioned
36. Presenter : 1. NM 2. Mentioned
37. Remarks by investigator (write strong/weak points of the programme :

APPENDIX-2

LIST OF THE PROGRAMMES TELECAST BETWEEN FEBRUARY 2 TO MARCH 2, 1988

Date	*Programmes*	*Agency*	*Duration*
2.2.88	1. Motivation	EMRC, Hyderbad	18
2.2.88	2. Social Behaviour & communication	Australia	30
3.2.88	3. Agriculture Growth In India	EMRC, Ahmedabad	19
3.2.88	4. Village Water supply	EMRC, Poona	10
3.2.88	5. Why Should A Collective Farm Need A Bear	USSR	28
5.2.88	6. Zero Second	DECU	30
5.2.88	7. Journey Through The Solar System-Pioneer-Saturn Encounter	USA	29
8.2.88	8. Optical Alignment-II	AVRC, Roorkee	25
8.2.88	9. Triaxial Compression Test	TTTI	20
8.2.88	10. Computer Devices	EMRC, Ahmedabad	10
9.2.88	11. Eklavya	EMRC, Hyderabad	18
9.2.88	12. The Ethology of Human Beings	Australia	30
9.2.88	13. Understanding of Media-An Introduction	EMRC, Poona	10
10.2.88	14. Arid Zone Ecology Phase-II Plant Extraction	EMRC, Ahmedabad	17
10.2.88	15. Deserts Bats	AVRC, Jodhpur	18
10.2.88	16. The New Biology Exhibition	MCRC, Delhi	20
11.2.88	17. Engineered Brick Masonry	AVRC, Madras	20
11.2.88	18. Usar Land Development	MCRC, Delhi	28
11.2.88	19. Plain and Plateaux	UK	09
12.2.88	20. The Space Ladder	DECU	13
12.2.88	21. Journey Through The Solar System Voyagar	USA	29

II-Saturn Encounter

12.2.88	22. The Sun as a Nuclear Reactor-Energy From Space	FRG	12
13.2.88	23. Cinematic Eye-Jules And Jins	USA	29
13.2.88	24. Language and Gesture-V	EMRC, Poona	24
15.2.88	25. Optical Alignment-III	AVRC, Roorke	34
15.2.88	26. Let There be Light	AVRC, Calcutta	21
16.2.88	27. Logic of Distance Education	EMRC, Hyderabad	—21
16.2.88	28. Educational Technology	MCRC, Delhi	22
16.2.88	29. Concepts of Sociology	MCRC, Delhi/ AVRC, Madurai	11
17.2.88	30. Arid Zone Ecology	EMRC, Ahmedabad	21

Phase-II

Mouse, But Not Mickey

17.2.88	31. With Net and Trap	FRG	28
18.2.88	32. Rural Water Supply	AVRC, Madras	18
18.2.88	33. Modern Irrigation System	EMRC, Poona	18
18.2.88	34. Soil Tillage in Dryland Agriculture	AVRC, Hyderabad	22
19.2.88	35. The Universe Part-I	EMRC, Poona	24
19.2.88	36. Journey Through The Solar System-Uranus, Neptune, Pluto and Beyond	USA	29
20.2.88	37. Demonstration on Indian Music-II Alaapana	EMRC, Hyderabad	25
20.2.88	38. Language of Music	MCRC, Delhi	29
22.2.88	39. Unification of Physics With Life	EMRC, Poona	20
22.2.88	40. Scientific Knowledge	AVRC, Calcutta	18
22.2.88	41. New Ideas in Science and Technology	USSR	18
23.2.88	42. Correspondence Courses	EMRC, Hyderabad	17
23.2.88	43. University of Poona-Solving Educational Problems	EMRC, Poona	22

23.2.88	44. Note Taking And Note Making	AVRC, Calcutta	18
24.2.88	45. Arid Zone Ecology	EMRC, Ahmedabad	23
	Phase-II		
	Fruits From Dryland		
24.2.88	46. How to Harvest Twice	FRG	29
25.2.88	47. Rural Sanitation	AVRC, Madras	18
25.2.88	48. Prescription for Health	Canada	23
25.2.88	49. War on Rats	AVRC, Hyderabad	17
26.2.88	50. Rain Making	EMRC, Ahmedabad	19
26.2.88	51. Remote Sensing Application and Technology	EMRC, Poona	20
26.2.88	52. Hurricane Below	USA	15
27.2.88	53. Demonstration on Indian Music-II	EMRC, Hyderabad	29
27.2.88	54. Folk Instruments of India	AIMS	26
29.2.88	55. Scientific Methods	AVRC, Calcutta	18
29.2.88	56. Treatment of Raw Water for Drinking Purposes	TTTI	17
29.2.88	57. University Round Up	PTI	19
1.3.88	58. Defence Mechanisms	EMRC, Hyderabad	17
	Part-II Conflict		
1.3.88	59. The Origin and Adaptiveness of Behaviour	Australia	35
2.3.88	60. The Brain	MCRC, Delhi	20
2.3.88	61. Some Aspects of Cancer Research In India	EMRC, Ahmedabad	22
2.3.88	62. Endoscopy-The Inner View	EMRC, Poona	11

MSA 02

1. Coder's name :
2. Date and time : Day
Programme no. : 1 2 3 4 5 (Filler)
10. Please code for one minute

Mts	*Shots*	*Treatment*	*Sound*	*Setting*	*Message Elements*	*Remarks*
1	1 2 3 4	1 2 3 4 5 6	1 2 3 4	1 2 3 4	1 2 3 4	
2	1 2 3 4	1 2 3 4 5 6	1 2 3 4	1 2 3 4	1 2 3 4	
3	1 2 3 4	1 2 3 4 5 6	1 2 3 4	1 2 3 4	1 2 3 4	
4	1 2 3 4	1 2 3 4 5 6	1 2 3 4	1 2 3 4	1 2 3 4	
5	1 2 3 4	1 2 3 4 5 6	1 2 3 4	1 2 3 4	1 2 3 4	
6	1 2 3 4	1 2 3 4 5 6	1 2 3 4	1 2 3 4	1 2 3 4	
7	1 2 3 4	1 2 3 4 5 6	1 2 3 4	1 2 3 4	1 2 3 4	
8	1 2 3 4	1 2 3 4 5 6	1 2 3 4	1 2 3 4	1 2 3 4	
9	1 2 3 4	1 2 3 4 5 6	1 2 3 4	1 2 3 4	1 2 3 4	
10	1 2 3 4	1 2 3 4 5 6	1 2 3 4	1 2 3 4	1 2 3 4	
11	1 2 3 4	1 2 3 4 5 6	1 2 3 4	1 2 3 4	1 2 3 4	
12	1 2 3 4	1 2 3 4 5 6	1 2 3 4	1 2 3 4	1 2 3 4	
13	1 2 3 4	1 2 3 4 5 6	1 2 3 4	1 2 3 4	1 2 3 4	
14	1 2 3 4	1 2 3 4 5 6	1 2 3 4	1 2 3 4	1 2 3 4	
15	1 2 3 4	1 2 3 4 5 6	1 2 3 4	1 2 3 4	1 2 3 4	
16	1 2 3 4	1 2 3 4 5 6	1 2 3 4	1 2 3 4	1 2 3 4	
17	1 2 3 4	1 2 3 4 5 6	1 2 3 4	1 2 3 4	1 2 3 4	
18	1 2 3 4	1 2 3 4 5 6	1 2 3 4	1 2 3 4	1 2 3 4	
19	1 2 3 4	1 2 3 4 5 6	1 2 3 4	1 2 3 4	1 2 3 4	
20	1 2 3 4	1 2 3 4 5 6	1 2 3 4	1 2 3 4	1 2 3 4	
21	1 2 3 4	1 2 3 4 5 6	1 2 3 4	1 2 3 4	1 2 3 4	
22	1 2 3 4	1 2 3 4 5 6	1 2 3 4	1 2 3 4	1 2 3 4	
23	1 2 3 4	1 2 3 4 5 6	1 2 3 4	1 2 3 4	1 2 3 4	
24	1 2 3 4	1 2 3 4 5 6	1 2 3 4	1 2 3 4	1 2 3 4	
25	1 2 3 4	1 2 3 4 5 6	1 2 3 4	1 2 3 4	1 2 3 4	
26	1 2 3 4	1 2 3 4 5 6	1 2 3 4	1 2 3 4	1 2 3 4	
27	1 2 3 4	1 2 3 4 5 6	1 2 3 4	1 2 3 4	1 2 3 4	
28	1 2 3 4	1 2 3 4 5 6	1 2 3 4	1 2 3 4	1 2 3 4	
29	1 2 3 4	1 2 3 4 5 6	1 2 3 4	1 2 3 4	1 2 3 4	
30	1 2 3 4	1 2 3 4 5 6	1 2 3 4	1 2 3 4	1 2 3 4	
31	1 2 3 4	1 2 3 4 5 6	1 2 3 4	1 2 3 4	1 2 3 4	
32	1 2 3 4	1 2 3 4 5 6	1 2 3 4	1 2 3 4	1 2 3 4	
33	1 2 3 4	1 2 3 4 5 6	1 2 3 4	1 2 3 4	1 2 3 4	
34	1 2 3 4	1 2 3 4 5 6	1 2 3 4	1 2 3 4	1 2 3 4	
35	1 2 3 4	1 2 3 4 5 6	1 2 3 4	1 2 3 4	1 2 3 4	

MSA 03

MESSAGE SYSTEM ANALYSIS OF INSAT COUNTRYWIDE CLASSROOM

Programme Coding Key

Video Shots

1. Close up
2. Mid shot
3. Long/very long shot
4. Caption/special effect

Programme Treatment

1. Demonstration (real and simulated)
2. Lecture/Expert speaking/illustrated lecture
3. Panel Discussion/Interview/Press Conference/Quiz
4. Documentary (narrative, simulated, actual)
5. Drama (with real actors/puppats/animation/story)
6. Cultural/Musical Performance

Use of Sound

1. Voice on the vision
2. Voice off the vision
3. Music on/off the screen
4. Original songe effects/special effects

Setting of the programme

1. Home/Indoor/Office
2. Classroom/Seminar/Conference Room/Hall
3. Laboratory/Factory/Industrial/Scientific Setting
4. Related Field Location/Natural Surrounding

Programme Objective

1. Concept/Idea/Theory/Law—discussed and identified
2. Concept/Idea/Theory/Low—recapitulated/reinforced
3. Subsequent New Concepts/Ideas/Theory/Law Discussed and Identified
4. Idea finally summarised and Overviewed

REFERENCES

Barcus, F. Earle (1969). Education in Content Analysis, In *The Analysis of Communication Content.* George Gerbner *et al.* (eds) New York : John Wiley and Sons Inc. pp. 539-54.

Berelson, B. (1952). *Content Analysis in Communication Research.* New York : Free Press.

Bruce, Cecilia (1985). *A Bird's Eye-View of Ahmedabad—Pij TV Programmes* (Kheda Communication Project). Ahmedabad : Development and Educational Communication Unit.

Chauhan, Harminder Kaur (1980). "Content Analysis and Viewer's Reaction Towards Pariwaran Layce Programme Telecast from Jullundur Amritsar Television Station". Ludhiana : Punjab Agricultural University. (Unpublished Ph.D. thesis).

George, Gerbner *et al.* (eds) (1969). *The Analysis of Communication Content.* New York : John Wiley and Sons.

George, Gerbner (1969). Toward "Cultural Indicators" : The Analysis of Mass Mediated Public Message Systems. In George Gerbner *et al.* (eds). *The Analysis of Communication Content.* New York : John Wiley, pp. 123-32.

Joshi, Ila (1987). Content Analysis of "Country-wide Classroom"—November 1987. Ahmedabad : EMRC, Gujarat University.

Joshi, S.R., M. Shah and R. Miṣra (1984). What went on Air (Kheda Communication Project). Ahmedabad : Space Applications Centre.

Krippendorff, Klaus (1980). *Content Analysis : An Introduction to its Methodology.* Beverly Hills, London : Sage Publications.

Misra, Radha (1984). Images and Messages (Kheda Communication Project). Ahmedabad: Space Applications Centre.

Misra, Radha (1985). Children's Programmes : What's in it? (Kheda Communication Project). Ahmedabad : Development and Educational Communication Unit.

Mody, Bella (1977). SITE Message System Analysis. Ahmedabad : Space Applications Centre.

Mody, Bella (1979). Programming for SITE. *Journal of Communication* Vol . 29 (4) : pp. 90-98.

North, R.C. *et al.* (1963). *Content Analysis : A Handbook with Applications for the Study of International Crisis.* Evanston : North-Western University.

Prasad, B.K. (ed.) (1986). *Mass Communication in India : An Annotated Bibliography 1978-80.* New Delhi : Indian Institute of Mass Communication.

Shah, Manjari (1984). "Second Channel" of Ahmedabad. Ahmedabad : Development and Educational Communication Unit.

Stone, P.J. *et al.* (1966). *The General Inquirer : A Computer Approach to Content Analysis.* Cambridge : MIT Press.

6

EDUCATIONAL IMPACT OF DISTANCE EDUCATION LEARNING

An Evaluation of Telesymposium via APPLE on Satellite Communication

BINOD C. AGRAWAL

INTRODUCTION

AMONG SEVERAL experiments, under the 'APPLE Applications Programme' a 'video lecture course' in the form of a telesymposium was organised between August 10-13, 1983. For this purpose, video lectures on satellite communications and related subjects were produced with the help of communications experts at Space Applications Centre, Ahmedabad. These video lectures were aimed at providing advance learning in satellite communications to engineering students and other professionals.

The course was intended for the final year undergraduate and postgraduate students of electronics and communications engineering. The 'TV course' package consisted of two sets of material. These were : (a) lecture notes and (b) video lectures. The lecture notes were provided to the participants in advance so they could read these notes before attending the video lectures. In addition, two way voice link facility was made available for "after video lecture" discussion between participants and the lecturers. This telesymposium is first of its kind in India for an advance level of electronics/communication teaching. It involved APPLE Satellite which provided nation-wide reach, a group of communication experts, production facilities and organisational arrangements for viewing the programmes. The transmission and reception of the telesymposium in this respect involved a complex organisational, managerial and technological system.

The four days telesymposium demanded high degree of coordination and planning at five receiving centres like ISRO Satellite Centre,

Bangalore; Space Applications Centre, Ahmedabad; Tata Institute of Fundamental Research, Bombay; Post and Telegraph Earth Station, Chingalpet, Madras; and Delhi Earth Station, Delhi. The participants came to view the TV programmes at these viewing centres. Analysis and understanding of the organisational aspects and coordination of such a telesymposium seems to be very important for future planning of similar video courses.

As a part of the total effort, an evaluation of telesymposium was planned. The evaluation among other things, aimed at measuring the impact of distance learning and the organisational aspects of giving such courses via satellite. The evaluation consisted of two parts. In the first part, the comprehension and liking of the video lectures were studied. In the second part, knowledge gain as a result of TV viewing in subject matter areas was measured.

Evaluation Objectives

1. To measure knowledge gain as a result of participation in telesymposium in the areas of Satellite Communications, Earth Stations, Base Band Techniques, APPLE, INSAT and Direct Reception System (DRS).
2. To observe the reactions and responses of the participants towards telesymposium, and television programmes.
3. To study the organisational aspects of the telesymposium for future planning.

Evaluation Design

Due to technical constraints and the nature of the course, the potential participants in the course were limited to final year undergraduate and postgraduate students. In order to measure the impact of TV in terms of knowledge gain, it was considered desirable to use 'pre' and 'post' test method of evaluation. As the TV course was of short duration, it was felt unnecessary to have a "control group". Hence, the tests were administered only to "experimental group" or telesymposium participants. Knowledge gain has been measured as follows :

$$P_1 - P_0 = G$$

Whereas P_1 = mean score of the post-test knowledge
P_0 = mean score of the pre-test knowledge
G = mean score difference or knowledge gain

Sample

In all five cities, namely, Ahmedabad, Bangalore, Bombay, Delhi and Madras, the students of the local Engineering College/Institute were expected to participate in the telesymposium. In Ahmedabad, the students of Engineering, Gujarat University attended the telesymposium. In Bangalore, the students and faculty of Indian Institute of Sciences participated in the telesymposium. Due to heavy rain and long distance between Tata Institute of Fundamental Research (the venue for viewing TV) and Indian Institute of Technology, Bombay, none could attend the telesymposium. In Delhi, the students and faculty of the Indian Institute of Technology, Kanpur and Delhi participated in the telesymposium. In Madras, the undergraduate students of Indian Institute of Technology attended the TV course.

Table 6.1 provides the details of total number of participants who attended the whole telesymposium. Table 6.2 shows the attrition rate (dropout rate from pre and post test) of the sample which was highest in Madras (87.9%) and lowest in Delhi (11.5%). On an average, the attrition rate of sample was 52.6 per cent. The distance between IIT Madras and Chinglepet being about 70 kilometers had dampning affect on the students' participation even when IIT Madras provided bus service for this purpose. Both in Madras and Bangalore, there was clash between the timings of telesymposium and class lectures which affected the participation.

All participants present on the first day before starting the video lectures filled the "pre-test" questionnaire. All participants present on the last day filled the "post-test" questionnaire. Only 61 persons having filled both pre and post-test questionnaires constituted the sample of the evaluative study. However, while discussing the suggestions for improvement, the responses of all the 76 participants who filled the post-test questionnaire have been taken into consideration. From all accounts, the dropout participants seemed to be randomly distributed that too due to serious local problem in Madras and Bombay.

Table 6.1 : Number of Participants who Filled both Pre and Post test Questionnaires by Viewing Centres

Location	*Pre-test*	*Post-test*	*Filled both Questionnaires*
Ahmedabad	38	36	26
Bangalore	13	6	6
Delhi	34	32	27
Madras	31	2	2
Total	116	76	61

Table 6.2 : Showing Sample Attrition Rate by Viewing Centre

Location	*Pre-test*	*Post-test*	*Differences*	*Attrition rate in per cent*
Ahmedabad	38	36	2	14.1
Bangalore	13	6	7	36.8
Delhi	34	32	2	11.5
Madras	31	2	29	87.9
Total/Average	116	76	40	52.6

Data Collection

Two distinct methods of data collection were employed for the evaluation of the telesymposium. The quantitative survey data with the help of a questionnaire were collected, whereas qualitative data were collected through participant observation.

Survey

The questionnaire developed for the collection of pre-test survey data included 29 knowledge items and questions related to socio-economic background of the participants. In post-test questionnaire, 15 additional items were included relating to telesymposium viewing condition, level of participation, general course organisation, video lecture comprehension, format and post video lecture two way audio interaction. All the knowledge questions were evolved in consultation with the experts and course director who prepared the lecture notes and gave video lectures.

Both the pre and post test questionnaires were pre-tested and revised in which 29 knowledge items were randomly distributed in the final questionnaire to minimize any patterned answering.

The 29 knowledge items for the purpose of analysis were grouped into four broad subject areas. These were 'Earth Stations' (nine items), 'Satellite Communications' (eight items), Base Band Techniques (six items) and 'APPLE, INSAT and DRS' (six items). Each item was assigned a score of zero for an incorrect answer and one for a correct answer. For each subject, a 'mean score' percentage was calculated as follows :

$$\text{Mean Score Percentage} = \frac{\text{total score of a subject} \times 100}{\text{number of items} \times \text{sample size}}$$

The pre-test questionnaire was administered half an hour prior to the actual TV telecast on August 1983. It took about 15-25 minutes for the participants to fill the questionnaire. Similalry on August 13, 1983 just after the completion of the TV telecast the post-telecast questionnaire was administered to the participants.

Observation

In order to have a qualitative and an indepth understanding of the participants' reaction and response to the telesymposium an "Observation Sheet" was developed. This observation sheet included ten items on "behavioural response", four items on "emotional response" and three items on 'participation'. Three observations were made the first five minutes after the beginning of the session, second at mid point, and third five minutes before the end of the video lecture session. Nine researchers at Ahmedabad (four), Delhi (two) and Bangalore (three) chose about five to six participants each for observing their behaviour during the telesymposium.

Social Characteristics of the Participants

The sample for this study consisted of 57 males and four females. The male/female ratio in the sample is quite comparable to what one will find in the technical institutions of higher learning in India today. Majority of the participants were students (53 or 86.9%) as this course was designed for the students. The remaining 8 or 13.1 per cent participants were teachers/engineers with an exception of one laboratory assistant of Indian Institute of Sciences, Bangalore. The students belonged to both under-graduate and postgraduate classes. However, the majority were under-graduate (32 or 52.5%) followed by postgraduate (21 or 34.4% see Table 6.3). Professional engineers were having both level of degrees.

Media exposure of the participants was very high. On an average, three fourth of the participants in the sample of 61 were exposed to TV, radio and read newspapers and magazines. As TV has not been introduced in the city of Ahmedabad yet, about 54 per cent of them had not viewed TV. Otherwise, more than 85 per cent of the participants were exposed to various kinds of mass media (see Table 6.4).

Except four or 6.6 per cent every participant had provided information on approximate monthly family income. It was observed that the monthly family income of 46 or 70.5 per cent participants was one thousand rupees. This average income is much above the average national income thereby showing that the participants belonged to "rich" upper income group. The remaining 14 or 23 per cent fall within the category of Rs. 500 to 1000 monthly income group which is still higher income than

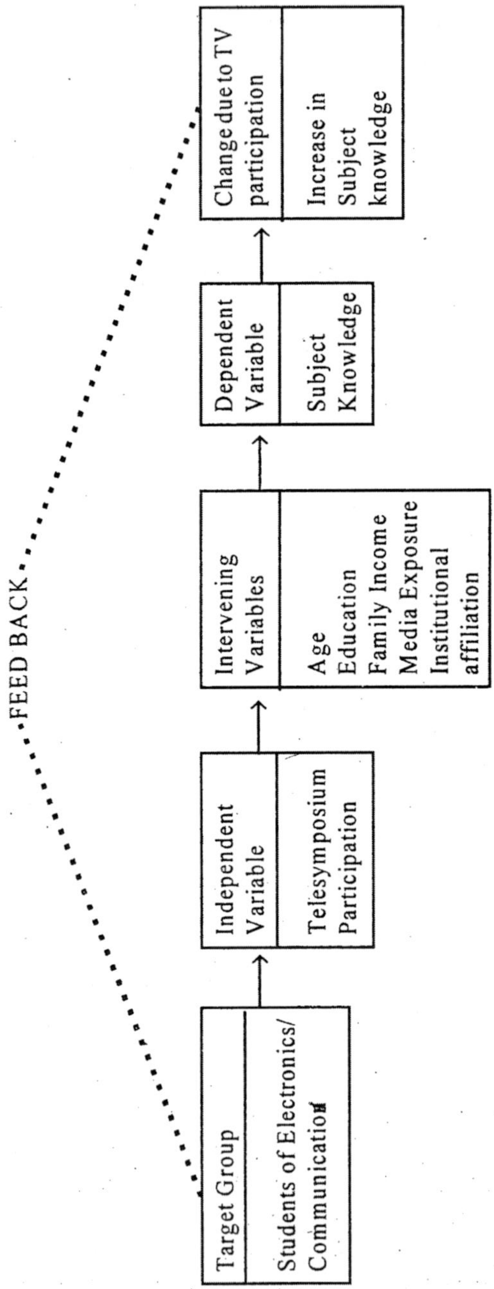

Fig. 6.1 : Conceptual Framework to Measure the Impact of Telesymposium.

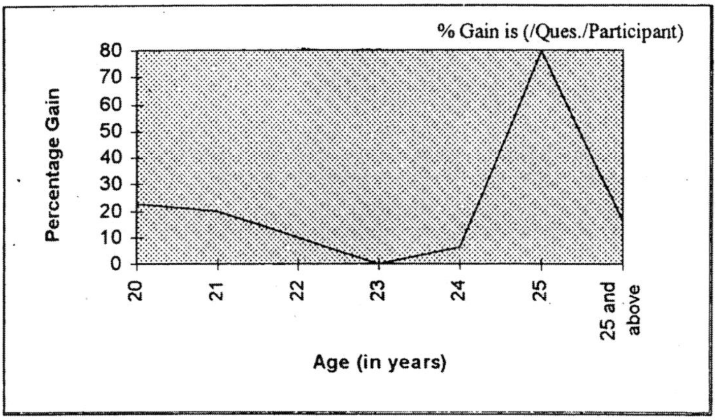

Fig. 6.2 : Knowledge Gain of Participants (Age-wise).

the national average. The economic characteristics of the participants indicated that they all belonged to the high income group of the country.

Table 6.3 : Percentage Distribution of Participants by Education and Profession.

Profession/ Education	*Undergraduate*	*Postgraduate*	*Total*
Students	52.5	34.4*	86.9
	(32)	(21)	(53)
Professionals	1.6**	11.5	13.1
	(1)	(7)	(8)
Total	54.1	45.9	100.00
	(33)	(28)	(61)

* It includes one Ph.D. students

** One laboratory assistant having a diploma

All figures are given in brackets

Higher Learning Through Television

The measurement of knowledge gain as a result of 'TV course' was one of the most important aspects of the evaluation. Conceptual framework to measure the impact of telesymposium on the participants is indicated in Figure 6.1. As indicated in Figure 6.2 age, education, family income per month, media exposure (in terms of radio listening, TV viewing and news/magazine reading) and institutional affiliation of the participants

Table 6.4 : Percentage of Media Exposure by Institutional Affiliation

Institution	*TV*		*Radio*		*Newspaper*		*Magazines*	
	Expo-sed	*Not Ex-posed*	*Expo-sed*	*Not Ex-posed*	*Expo-sed*	*Not Ex-posed*	*Expo-sed*	*Not Ex-posed*
College	46.1	53.9	92.6	7.4	88.5	11.5	80.8	19.2
	(12)	(14)	(24)	(2)	(23)	(3)	(21)	(2)
Institute	94.3	5.7	82.9	17.1	100.0	–	94.3	5.7
	(33)	(2)	(29)	(6)	(35)	–	(33)	(2)
Total Percentage	73.8	26.2	96.9	13.1	95.1	4.9	88.5	.11.5
	(45)	(16)	(53)	(8)	(58)	(3)	(54)	(7)

College includes L.D. Engineering College and Gujarat University Student, Ahmedabad. Institute includes IIT's of Kanpur, Delhi and Madras and Indian Institute of Science, Bangalore.

Note : Figures in brackets show frequency.

(locations of the technical institutions) have been treated as intervening variables, whereas subject knowledge was considered as dependent variable. The impact of telesymposium has been measured in terms of increase in subject knowledge as indicated earlier in four subjects areas namely 'Earth Stations', 'Satellite Communications', 'Base Band Techniques' and 'APPLE, INSAT, and DRS'.

Table 6.5 provides knowledge gain in four subject areas. On the whole, Table 6.5 indicates statistically significant gain in knowledge in all four subjects as a result of telesymposium participation and reading of lecture notes. Table 6.5 also shows that the highest knowledge gain was observed in the area of 'Satellite Communication' (27.5%) whereas the lowest knowledge gain was recorded on 'Earth Stations'. Two possible explanations for these variations can be offered.

The topics covered in earth stations provided very detailed and indepth information to the participants which might not have been absorbed by the participants in such a short period. The other reason could have been that the lecture based on practical experiences of the experts was too new material for the participants to grasp. On the other hand, subject like satellite communications was broad and some of the informations were known to the participants in which telesymposium helped clarifying the concepts. The same can be said about 'Base Band Techniques' presentation.

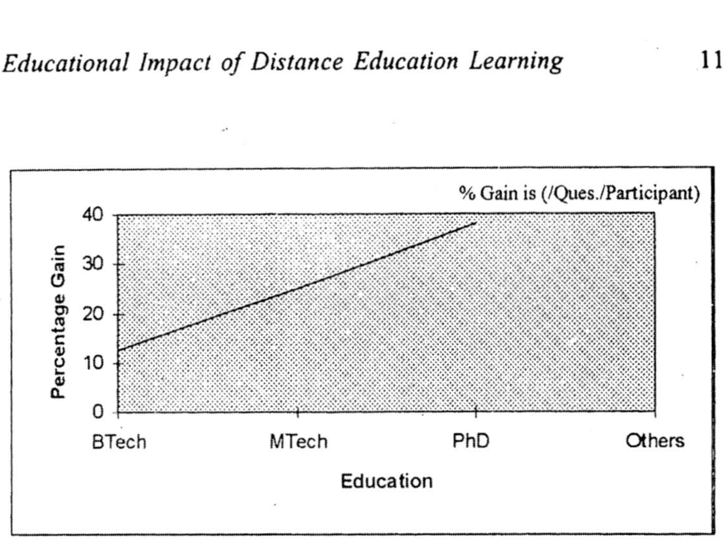

Fig. 6.3 : Knowledge Gain of Participants (Education-wise).

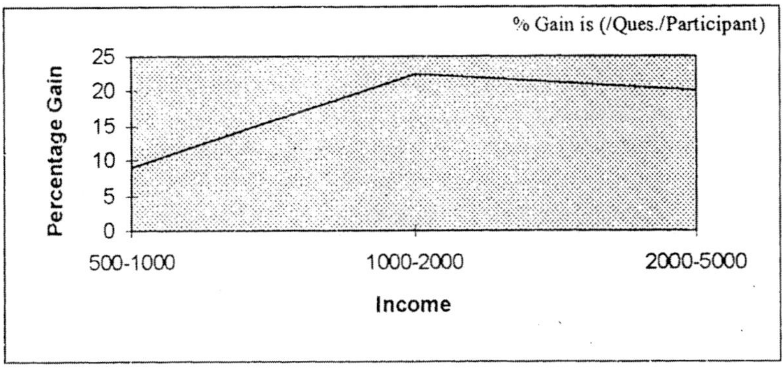

Fig. 6.4 : Knowledge Gain of Participants (Income-wise).

As gain in knowledge was found on all four subjects, it was felt that separate analysis for each item would not be of great importance. Hence, the intervening variables age, education and montly family income was utilized to analyse the total knowledge gain of the participants. Figure 6.2

Table 6.5 : Overall Percentage Knowledge Gain by Subject

Subject	*Post-test knolwedge*	*Pre-test knowledge*	*Knowledge gain*	*Value of Test*
Earth Stations	57.0	46.4	10.6	–3.653**
Satellite Communications	72.1	44.6	27.5	–5.885**
Base Band Techniques	52.1	39.6	12.5	–3.163**
APPLE, INSAT and DRS	64.4	46.7	18.3	–4.470**

** Significant at 0.01 level, sample size = 61

shows that knowledge gain was highest among those participants who were 25 years of age. There was zero gain at the age of 23 as indicated in the Figure 6.2 because there was no participant of this age group in the sample. At the same time, those participants who were above 25 years of age show decline in knowledge gain thereby indicating an inverse relationship between age and knowledge gain through TV course.

Figure 6.3 seems to indicate that there is a direct correlation between education of the participants and knowledge gain. This seems to be quite possible as it is expected that the participants having higher level of education would be able to absorb more from the lecture notes and TV course. Figure 6.4 shows that participants having monthly family income between Rs. 1000-2000 per month gained the most from the telesymposium, whereas the lowest gain was indicated by those participants whose family income was between Rs. 500-1000 per month. The 'higher income goups' gained more than participants of 'lower income group', they indicated a declining trend from the middle income group. The possible explanation for such a trend could be that the pressure for higher achievement might be greater in the homes of the "middle income group" participants.

One the whole Figures 6.2, 6.3 and 6.4 suggest that the younger participants studying at M. Tech level and belonging to Rs. 1000-2000 per month family income had gained maximum from the telesymposium participation and lecture notes. Having observed earlier that media exposure was above 85 per cent among the participants, this intervening variable was found not helpful in explaining the variations among the participants. Hence, no analysis is being presented.

Students and Knowledge Gain

A number of educationists and sociologists have argued that three intervening variables age, education and family income in the present context

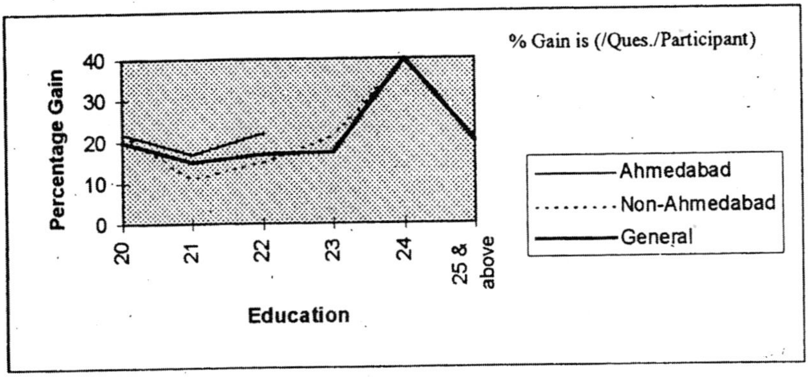

Fig. 6.5 : Knowledge Gain of Participants (Age-wise).

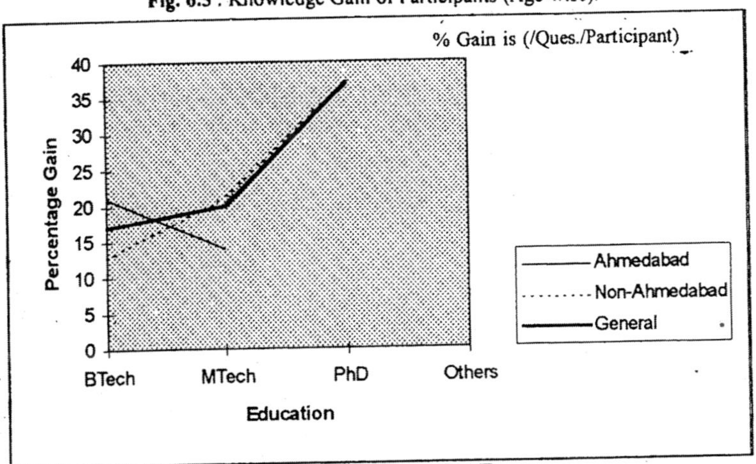

Fig. 6.6 : Knowledge Gain of Participants (Education-wise).

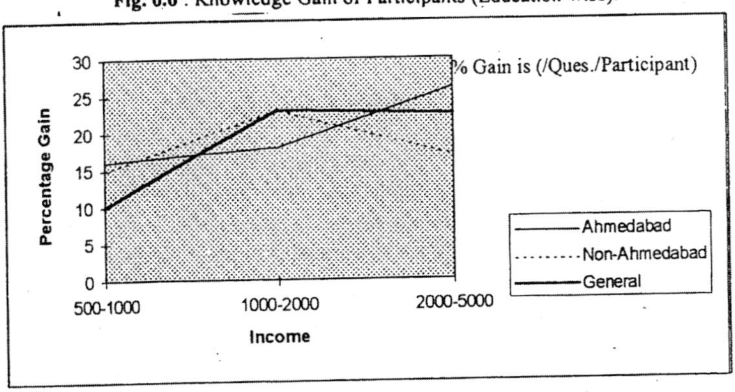

Fig. 6.7 : Knowledge Gain of Participants (Income-wise).

in no way can explain the factors responsible in determining the reasons of knowledge gain due to telesymposium participation. This argument has been advanced as it was felt that once a student was admitted to an institution of higher learning, he/she has already proved his/her scholastic achievement and therefore these intervening variables would not significantly affect the learning behaviour, especially the family income. Keeping this in view, the students belonging to L.D. Engineering College as opposed to the students of Indian Institute of Technology were thought would be at two levels of scholastic performances. Assuming that their performance levels were different, it was hypothesized that the institute students which include Indian Institute of Sciences, and Indian Institute of Technology would perform better than the college students of L.D. Engineering and space sciences students in terms of gain in knowledge from the participation in telesymposium. In order to do so, the participants of L.D. Engineering College (22 undergraduate and three space science post graduate students) and Indian Institute of Sciences and Indian Institute of Technology (10 undergraduate, 17 postgraduate and on Ph. D) were grouped separately for a comparative analysis.

Table 6.6 : Overall Percentage Knowledge Gain by Subject and Institutional Affiliation

Institution	*Earth Stations*	*Satellite Communication*	*Base Band Techniques*	*APPLE INSAT DRS*	*Sample Size*
College*	12.9	30.5	16.7	20.7	25
Institute**	12.3	28.1	10.1	19.1	28
Overall	12.6	29.3	13.2	19.8	53
'T' Values	–3.953***	–5.618***	–3.067***	–4.424***	

* College includes L.D. Engineering College, Ahmedabad and Space Science Students of Gujarat University.

** Institute includes students of Indian Institute of Technology, Delhi, Kanpur, Madras and Indian Institute of Sciences, Bangalore.

*** Significant at .01 level.

Table 6.6 indicates that the general pattern of knowledge gain as a result of telesymposium participation remained more or less similar among both groups of students. The highest knowledge gain (29.3 per cent) have been indicated in area of satellite communication, followed by APPLE, INSAT and DRS (19.8%) and other two subjects. The overall knowledge gain in all four subjects are statistically significant as indicated by T-test.

Further, comparative analysis of college and institute participants overall knowledge gain are presented in Figures 6.5, 6.6 and 6.7. Figure 6.5 provides age-wise knowledge gain, whereas Figure 6.6 provides education-wise knowledge gain and Figure 6.7 income-wise knowledge gain. In all the three figures, college participants especially those belonging to the age group 20-22 years, from family income of Rs. 500-1000 per month and studying at undergraduate level have shown higher overall knowledge gain when compared with Institute participants of the same category. However, Figure 6.6 shows that the postgraduate college participants gain less as compared to postgraduate institute participants. It may be mentioned that the three postgraduate college participants belonged to the first year space science course and that too three in number which is not comparable. Another interesting feature is indicated in Figure 6.7 college participants belonging to higher income group (Rs. 2000-5000) have gained higher than the institute participants.

It may be mentioned that the pre-test knowledge level in general was higher among institute participants as compared to college participants. But the overall knowledge gain as shown earlier is more or less similar in both cases. It seems that television as a medium of distance learning, atleast in this course, provided equal learning opportunity to the students. On the whole, the analysis presented so far, does not support the hypothesis that institute participants performed better in terms of gain in knowledge as compared to college participants as a result of their participation in telesymposium.

7

VIDEO USE IN DISTANCE EDUCATION

A South Asian Perspective

BINOD C. AGRAWAL

IN A small town of Andhra Pradesh (one of the larger states in India), the Andhra Pradesh Open University has created a study centre where a student, desiring to obtain a degree, is expected to come and watch video lessons, or listen to an audio cassette designed by a group of instructors sitting several hundred kilometres away in Hyderabad. Although it follows a multimedia approach most of the learning packages continue to be of print material. The Andhra Pradesh Open University in less than five years has grown manifold. From a modest enrolment of 7500 students in 1982, there are more than 55000 students studying in this university—a more than seven times expansion in less than five years. Same kind of expansion has been witnessed at the national level today. Uses of video in distance education must be analysed keeping such a perspective in view.

India is agog with the possibilities of distance education. Technological advances in video technology has further enhanced the South Asian hopes to use mass media on a cost effective basis for distance education. In the wake of video glare, the educators seem to be blinded to use other means of mass communication like radio and television. It is fairly evident from the way the University Grants Commission (India's highest body for university education) has decided to invest money in video technology for what is now popularly known as 'country-wide classroom' programme. Of course, it has a history of more than 10 years, when the Government of India, Ministry of Education and Welfare thought of investing more than 20 million Indian rupees for educational technology for the "spread of formal as well as non-formal education, making education relevant to the aspirations and needs of the community and reducing existing disparities sections of the population" (Report of the Task Force on Mass Communication and Educational Technology, 1983 : 1).

At present the climate is such that everybody and anybody who matters in the field of communications technology, education and mass media are busy propagating, advocating, recommending, insisting and supporting the use of video technology for solving most of the ills of education at various levels. What does it mean to an average teacher or student? In this race of video introduction for education, nobody seems to be questioning or worrying about the validity and utility of this assumption. What has emerged is, increasing use of video in distance education at various levels within India and in other countries of South Asia in which both hardware and software are largely imported.

In this paper my effort is to document some of the current thinking and uses of video in distance education, within the Indian sub-continent and its future implications. My focus is primarily country specific, because of the limited data availability of other South Asian countries. While doing so I shall try to examine the concept of distance education within the socio-economic and cultural milieu of South Asia. This analysis will focus on the method of video uses highlighting the multiple possibilities of uses of video due to variations in economic and technological developments even within a single country like India. Also built-in structural inequalities will be highlighted to emphasis the capital intensive nature of video use, thereby restricting mass use.

Distance Education : A South Asian Perspective

In November 1986 the Association of Indian Universities and the newly founded Indira Gandhi National Open University (IGNOU) organised a National Conference on Distance Education[1] at Gujarat University, Ahmedabad. It was one of the largest congregations of intellectuals and academicians to discuss the 'state of art', 'concept', 'form' and growing need of distance education in India. A large section in the conference was devoted to the 'Role of Media in Distance Education'. In more than one way, this was an earnest effort to bring together a group of professionals to discuss how distance education could be made meaningful, cost-effective, with the help of mass media, especially television both in transmission and non-transmission modes. The use of television in the non-transmission mode was identified as 'video use' in distance education. Even before I touch the use of video in distance education, it would

1. For details see the Proceedings of the National Conference on Distance Education, November 9 & 10, 1986 held at Gujarat University, Ahmedabad.

be worthwhile to discuss the very concept of distance education and its social ramifications in South Asia in general and in India in particular.

It was self-evident from papers and discussions of the November 1986 Conference that, the concept of distance education in its contemporary context is a borrowed idea from the Euro-American educational system by the Indian educationists. A review of more than 60 articles presented in the Conference and over 130 articles written earlier on distance education reflect the high degree to which the concept of distance education has been borrowed from the Euro-American educational system. It would not be out of place to indicate that the concept of distance education is in opposition to the ancient South Asian and Indian tradition of learning. "Conceptually the learning process is the result of the interaction of the teacher and the taught. In this sense, education is a 1:1 relationship. Should this relationship be physically a near close one? That was the ancient tradition—the Guru-Shishya relationship. And that is also the basis on which all systems of education have been developed." (Adiseshiah, 1986 : 7). The present education system in South Asia approximates this method of teaching and learning. In spite of formal educational systems imposed during the colonial period, the ancient educational system continues to play an important role in education.

Distance education has been associated with and has been thought to be 'correspondence education', in which course material is posted to the students who are expected to work and return the answers to the university and are expected to get further guidance if so desired. They are also expected to attend certain number of contact classes. They appear in an examination to obtain a degree. "The popularity of the course is such that the universities which run them make large sums of money (around Rs. 3—4 crores a year)[2] from it" (Adiseshiah, 1986 : 8). The additional support provided through radio and television has taken the shape of open university education, consciously borrowing from the model of the Open University, United Kingdom.

The Indian distance education as of today falls between these two forms of distance education though there are some efforts to break away from these two forms, and experiment with innovative methods specially in the area of adult education. In this respect distance education has been thought of "as a pragmatic approach of extending education to the millions of people for whom the word 'school' would remain a distant dream for years to come" (Shah, 1986 : 12). The exponents of distance education have strongly argued that educational needs of the growing

2. A crore is equivalent to 10 million.

population cannot be met through the existing educational system. Hence, there is a need for distance education. This argument is coupled with the view that learning is a life long process and there is a need for continuous education due to high rate of knowledge obsolescence.

Socio-Cultural Milieu of Distance Education

In the socio-cultural context of South Asia, distance education has turned into a 'class based' education for the 'elite' who are either aspiring to move upwards in the social hierarchy, or have missed the opportunity of acquiring appropriate degrees in the initial attempt. It would be desirable to elaborate this assertion in detail, to support a view which as conceived by the education planners and policy makers is in contrast with the very notion of distance education. According to the existing statistics about two thirds of India's population is illiterate. Little over one third of the population which is literate, not even 5 per cent of them can claim to have a degree of any kind (India, 1985, 1986 : 67).

Observations indicate that a large majority of students attending 'correspondence courses' or enrolled in the open university system in India belong to a social class who have already achieved a certain level of economic independence of one kind or the other and are trying for prosperity in which additional educational qualifications would act as a ladder for upward economic climbing. The fruits of distance education are being devoured by this class who are a minority. The open university system which is multiplying very fast in South Asia is also going to be no different from the correspondence courses in spite of the professed policy of providing education to the under-privileged. It is for this reason that there is a very strong argument that, "distance education is not to be seen as a poor relation or a distant cousin of the formal system... If the formal system has served the society fruitfully, so does the system of distance education hope to do" (Agrawal, 1986 : 2).

In a nation wide study on the video penetration and its socio-cultural implication, some interesting results surfaced regarding the other uses of video apart from "commercial film" viewing on video.[3] A series of

3. For details, see Indian Space Research Organisation (ISRO) sponsored study in collaboration with five social scientists entitled "Communication Revolution : Socio-cultural Implications of Video Technology in India". This study was initiated in 1985-86 and is in the process of completion. For this study, samples were drawn from five regions of the country and within each region, respondents were selected from urban and rural areas. The total sample was approximately 750 respondents. Similarly, more than 200 video shopkeepers, librarians and video parlour owners were also interviewed. Some of the trends indicated here are based on the preliminary findings of the study.

questions were asked to video viewers regarding the potential of video for education and development. These were mostly attitudinal questions to gauge the potentiality to video use in the non-formal, adult, class room and distance education. More than two third of the video viewers considered it to be both as a means of education and entertainment. Similarly, about three-fourth of the respondents thought that video has high educational potentiality. The respondents also feel that the use of video in educational process will effect teacher-student relationship though there is no hint about direction of this change.

It must be mentioned that none of the respondents had reported that they were students or teachers of distance education nor did the video libraries report having educational video tapes for rental. So while the viewers thought of positive use of video in education, the video libraries did not find it profitable to rent educational tapes. No doubt there are not many educational programmes on video available for general circulation in South Asia. Its absence in more than one way tells the gap that exists between the belief and reality, though educational programmes were preferred to be viewed on video than in cinema or TV in transmission mode by the respondents. Video has been thought of as a "boon" for Asian and African countries by more than three-fourth of the respondents, thereby reflecting a very high degree of acceptability of video as an educational tool.

Use of Video in Distance Education

The theoretical discussion in South Asia centering around the use of video, is no different than what one would have expected in countries like Japan, Canada, United Kingdom, the United States and several other countries of this kind. Video use provides flexibility, learning at convenience, at a pace desired by the learner, and control over the medium.

"Not only can the student watch *when* she wants but *as often* and with as many *pauses* or partial *replays* as necessary" (Brown 1984 : 44). The basic assumption in this kind of video use is an inherently individualistic learning approach, emanating from a cultural tradition and a techno-social development of a consumer economy. All these conditions can be fulfilled by a very small elite minority in South Asia, whose transnational connections will help bridge technological gaps, although it puts them on indefinite psychological inferiority and technological dependency.

In a "collective" culture such a technology whether in education or entertainment has a limited role to play until it goes through 'social indigenization' apart from 'technological indigenization'. Adaptation of video as a means for domestic and community entertainment reflects this process. The moot question is whether video would get indigenised for distance education.

The other question is as to who can afford to use video for individual learning in South Asia? The obvious answer is a very small minority. It is precisely this reason that has forced distance educators to think of restrictive uses of video in distance education. The initial example described earlier of Andhra Pradesh Open University indicated that the video has been a multiplier of good teachers for a larger reach. Typically a contact class is like a regular class in which students watch a video programme collectively (Narayana Reddy, 1986 : 17). In exceptional cases students are able to take video tapes at home for viewing. Efforts have been made to minimise such possibilities by choosing a technical system like U-matic three-quarter video cassette recorder so that the half inch VHS tapes cannot be viewed on this system. Several such methods are being evolved in other institutions of distance education to minimize 'misuse' of video cassette recorders.

A little over a million video cassette recorders that are available within India are being used for viewing commercial films on video. Once in a while an educational programme of foreign origin is also viewed by young children. In several training centres, video viewing is becoming popular among trainees for demonstration purposes. There are reports that some of the private institutions are in the process of acquiring video software from other countries to supplement their technical education programmes. Given the size and number of students, video use in distance education is still negligible.

There are several plans to produce video software in India for distance education. Under the 'country-wide classroom' programme, initially six centres were selected within the university system for the production of video programmes aimed for undergraduate students, in the English language.

Since August 1985, twice a day, for an hour, these programmes are telecast through the Indian National Satellite (INSAT) system. The programmes are basically aimed at enriching the students. In the absence of any evaluative study it is difficult to assess the programme effects on the undergraduate students. From the data available of the existing receiving system in the 5000 odd colleges it is clear that the reach is still very limited. The content analysis reflects that a good deal of the programmes telecast so far have been produced outside India, in English speaking countries like

England. The analysis of letters received from viewers, show that these programmes are being viewed by unintended target groups like housewives, high school students and working people.

The University Grants Commission is in the process of expanding the country-wide classroom project both in reach and scope by providing to the colleges and by setting up new production centres to stimulate culture specific programme production. In addition the University Grants Commission is initiating the video production of 15 course packages. In the production of these programmes there is a great deal of discussion regarding cultural compatibility, reflection of social reality, and value oriented education. Other important projects being initiated by the University Grants Commission are educational television series for preschool children. In all these efforts emphasis is layed on community viewing of video instead of individual viewing.

There are two important issues that must be discussed here relating to the uses of video in distance education. These are mode of transmission of video programmes and the scope of these programmes. The production grammar of these programmes is such that it seems there is no conscious effort on the part of producers to keep in view, whether these programmes would be used in the transmission mode or would they be meant for the individual learners in non-transmission mode. In most cases, it is considered that the same can be used both in the transmission and non-transmission mode. Some serious thinking is required regarding this point. If it is to be used for individual learning then the distribution aspect must be taken into consideration. The existing video libraries may help quick distribution of educational programmes within the country, which already has a large marketing network. Also, distance education institutions can create systems for individual distribution on the pattern of the circulating library system.

At the moment under the broad heading of enrichment, programmes are telecast without seriously defining the target group or the educational aim of the programme. This has helped throwing a broad net of educational programmes for distance education. But then it is difficult to assess who is really getting the advantage of this effort : are they college students or students enrolled in the distance education programmes or non-students? Only after defining the target group can the scope of the potential user be visualised in order to decide whether a programme should be transmitted or could be used in non-transmission mode.

At the primary education level, efforts are also being made to transmit enrichment programmes for children in the age group of 5-12 years. Also, the teacher training programmes are being carried out in the same way. These programmes are currently transmitted in several Indian languages during the morning hours on school days for classroom viewing. All these programmes are pre-recorded video tapes telecast from a central location on time sharing basis. There is no effort at present to use video programmes in the non-transmission mode for individual children to view these programmes.

In other South Asian countries like Pakistan efforts are being made through the Open University system for video use in distance education. At the school level use of video seems to be very limited in South Asia. The issue which is hotly discussed in this regard is that until infrastructure facilities are provided, how can higher economic investments be made for video use in distance education.

The Future

A future scenario of the uses of video in distance education is spelt out in the 'Programme of Action, National Policy on Education, 1986' in India. In addition to the on going uses, this action plan envisages to use video in the schools. For this purpose, "The Electronics Trade and Technology Development Corporation (ET&T) has formulated a 'TELETEACH' project to prepare educational software on videotape. VCR's and viewing equipment would be provided in about 600 viewing centres to be established in schools this year. The Ministry has also identified certain subject areas in which educational software would be developed by ET&T" (Programme of Action 1986 : 181). The Action Plan also envisages to "provide a dedicated educational TV channel by 1991-92; create a dedicated satellite system for educational needs in the long term; expansion of in-house programme production facilities... curricular support material using non-broadcast methods..." (Programme of Action 1986 : 181). What it means is that there will be a manifold expansion of video use for education in India in both broadcast and non-broadcast modes. In the absence of any detailed information about other countries in South Asia, it is not possible to provide similar future scenarios. Moreover, the formation of the South Association for Regional Cooperation (SAARC) might open up the possibility of similar uses of video for distance education in other South Asian countries. It, seems that the technological thrust in education is increasing to equalise opportunities for education. My own hunch is that this will increase the gulf of educational opportunities between "educational haves" and "educational have-nots". A conclusion that to some is very obvious, but is hidden under the carpet in official discussions among educationists and educational planners. My humble suggestion would be that we must evolve means and methods to ensure that video use in education helps equalise opportunities rather than increase the existing gulf (Agrawal, 1986).

REFERENCES

Adiseshiah, Malcolm S. (1986). Some Thoughts on the Concepts and Forms of Distance Education. *University News*, New Delhi (special issue). Volume XXIV, No. 42, pp. 7-9.

Agrawal, Binod C. (1986). *Culture, Communication and Knowledge : The Structural Predicaments*. Ahmedabad : Development and Educational Communication Unit-ISRO.

Brown, Stephen (1984). Video Cassettes. In *The Role of Technology in Distance Education*. Ed.

Editor (1987). Over to Ahmedabad. *University News* (Special Issue). Volume XXIV, No. 42 : 2.

India (1985). India 1985 : A Reference 1986 Annual. New Delhi : Publications Division. Ministry of Information and Broadcasting, Government of India.

Narayana Reddy, C. (1986) Andhra Pradesh Open University. *University News* (Special Issue). Volume XXIV, No. 42, pp. 17-20.

Programme of Action (1986). Programme of Action. National Policy on Education 1986. New Delhi : Government of India, Ministry of Human Resource Development, Department of Education.

Report of the Task Force on Mass Communication and Educational Technology (1983). University Grants Commission, New Delhi.

8

TELEVISION STUDIES IN INDIA

The State of the Art

THE HISTORY of Indian Television is just about a quarter of a century old with its humble beginning in 1959. The Indian television known as Doordarshan (a literal translation of tele and vision; from a distance), went through the incubation process in radio, and after almost 16 years of radio cradle, it reached adolescence, to be an independent entity in 1976. The decade that followed saw its maturation and unprecedented expansion. Doordarshan today can claim to be one of the world's largest satellite based telecast system covering over a 500 million population of viewers on a terrestrial system of India's approximately 800 million people who also receive television signals through direct broadcast. The history of Indian television research, hence, is closely linked with the radio audience research, literally lifted from the British Broadcasting Corporation in colonial India, prior to its independence in 1947. While discussing the television studies in India, a historical perspective seems to be eminently important, as it has had remarkable influence on the structure, organisation, research topics and publication policies of the television studies that were conducted until recently. It is in this milieu that an attempt to present an analysis of the television research traditions is being made. One year Satellite Instructional Television Experiment (SITE) conducted during 1975-76 provides the marker point for presenting the review as a large number of television studies were conducted during this period. Accordingly the analysis will be presented in three parts. In the first part, all the pre-SITE studies strictly following audience research method will be discussed. In the second part, SITE research will be described and methods that were followed in SITE studies will be analysed. In the third part, those closely associated with television expansion in India and related studies will be touched upon. Broadly various television studies in each part will be discussed under three sub-heading. These are (a) formative, (b) process and (c) summative, although earlier it was discussed under five subheadings (Agrawal, 1981 a). In addition, it will touch upon management and advertising research—an aspect little known, but of immense importance and implications for communication researchers in the third world and else where.

Several, social science research traditions namely, Anthropology, Sociology, Extension Education, Education and Psychology significantly influenced the television researches in India. Each discipline's theoretical and methodological pre-occupations are reflected in majority of the studies. In almost every available SITE research document, it has been asserted that SITE research "was conceived as inter and multi discip-linary, involving many disciplines of social sciences" (Agrawal, 1976 a; 1977 b).

Figure 8.1 provides a graphic representation and the inter-linkages of disciplines, research types and time periods of television research.

Disciplines	Anthropology		
	Sociology		
	Extension Education		
	Education		
	Psychology		
Type of Research	Radio (1967-73)	SITE (1973-77)	Doordarshan (1977-)
Formative	No	Yes	Yes
Process	Yes	Yes	Yes
Summative	Yes	Yes	?

Figure 8.1 : Showing Research Discipline, Types and Time Periods.

Television Studies Under Radio Patronage

In the early years of television studies in India, three groups of social scientists who got involved were directly or indirectly connected with education. They exclusively devoted their energies to measure the effectiveness of television as a medium of instruction and social education. International agencies played an important role in promoting television research. Within two years after the introduction of television in India, the

Delhi School Television Project, was initiated to promote the use of television for formal education at the higher secondary level. This being, the first educational television programme it was amply supported and was evaluated .in its totality. An American sociologist Paul Neurath conducted the first evaluative study on the effects of television on the higher secondary school. His research vividly brought out the learning experience in conducting a television research in the formal system of education. Neurath's study was a regular sociological study, using a historical and documentary approach for describing the Delhi School Television project in its educational and cultural milieu. For measuring the effectiveness a survey design was followed, in which both experimental and controlled schools were selected for data collection. The conclusion were even much more cautious. "By and large the television schools did somewhat—better in the tests than did the non-television schools" (Neurath (ed.) : 62). While there is no clear indication that formative researches were conducted for evaluating the need of the students, existing documents indicate that the production team in collaboration with content matter experts (in this case educationists) carefully examined the needs of the students before deciding the topics. However, very little effort was made to study the suitability of formats, information load and methods of presentation. Also, no researches were conducted related to language suitability as the programmes were to be telecast within a limited area of Delhi. Several feedback methods were evolved, but these were mostly in the form of weekly or monthly reports to be mechanically filled by the concerned teachers and schools for the use of higher-ups. How did the feedback studies influence the television production and modify the existing system of transmission is not known. But, there are good indications that the "feedback" reports were seriously considered by production and transmission authorities. On the whole, educational television was closely linked with the related researches, which over a period of time lost its importance once the television transmission became routinised and international agencies supporting the project withdrew from the scene. Few theses in the department of education were also attempted, a venture that still continues. The educationists were and are seriously wanting to measure micro-level knowledge gain, as a result of television viewing. Also, they were looking at the potential use of television in improving the quality of television and to act as an aid in the education process.

Another television project that attracted the attention of agricultural extension researchers was *Krishi Darshan.* Krishi Darshan (literally means agricultural vision) was an attempt for the use of television for the instruction of farmers to improve agricultural productivity. It was again a pilot project initiated after seven years of television introduction in India on January 26, 1967. Twice a week, about half an hour time was devoted for the telecast of special agricultural programmes to provide latest information on farming technology. Since then this programme continues to be telecast with increased frequency for a large part of the country. Between 1967 and 1972 a series of process and summative studies were conducted to measure the effects of agricultural programmes. The basic assumption in all these studies had been that external information provided through television would change the attitude and supplement knowledge gain of the farmers and would help in the adoption of agricultural innovations. The single most important theoretical postulation that influenced all these studies was the five stage "adoption model" (Rogers 1962). Even after the publication of several articles and books rejecting the five stages of the adoption model of innovations, television studies related to agricultural programmes followed the same model. American influence on television studies was most discernable and prominent in this period. To some extent the influence is continuing. Without exception, television studies related to agricultural programmes followed the survey approach. In most of these studies the 'before' and 'after' experimental design was used. Few process studies that were conducted were essentially a part of the larger summative evaluation. These studies in general provided, insights for future programme, production and planning. The most important gains from these studies were related to the operations and maintenance of community television for rural development an idea which has received great attention in India. The researches related to community television continues to draw attention in India as it is believed that individual television ownership will remain a privilege of a few.

During this period some efforts were also made to study the viewers reaction on day-to-day basis, but majority of these studies end up looking at the mechanics of television operation, specially in community television viewing situation. Historical records do not support the view that European research models especially the methods and techniques used in BBC were initiated or even used in the process studies. As Indian television during this period did not carry any commercial advertisements, marketing researches related to television advertisements were rare, though there is evidence to support the view that advertising agencies were wanting to use television for advertisements based on these studies. Some studies were carried out by the Audience Research Unit of All-India Radio (AIR) to measure the viewership and programme preferences. It would not

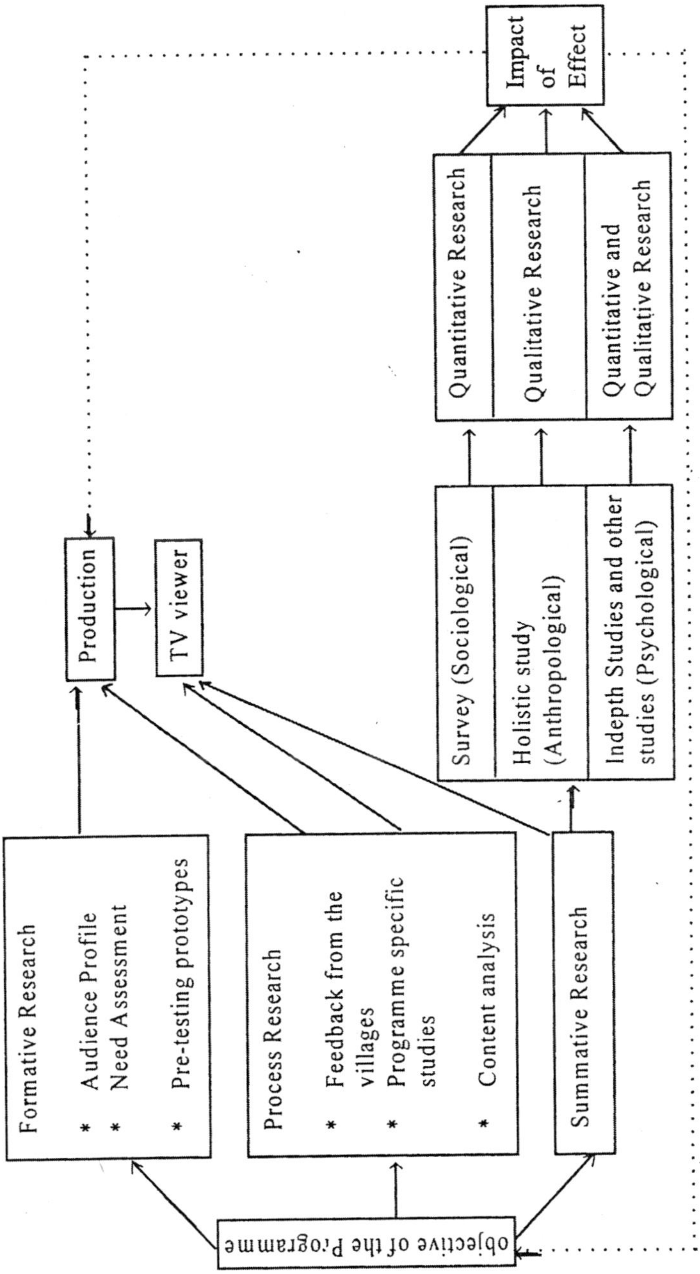

Fig. 8.2 : Conceptual Frame for Communications Research in SITE

be far from the truth to say that two divergent views were in vogue at this juncture in the Indian television studies. On one side, a serious effort to use communication researches for improving the quality of television production and to study the effects. On the other side an aversion towards conducting any television study. These two divergent views are somewhat converged in the latter part which will be discussed.

Television Studies during SITE

One of the significant aspects of Satellite Instructional Television Experiment (SITE) related to a conscious decision on the part of experimenters was to have a total evaluation of the project including social evaluation. The social evaluation was the responsibility of the Indian side, in this Indo-American joint venture. It is precisely for this reason, apart from other reasons, all efforts were made by the Indian Space Research Organisation (one of the main partners of the experiment) to provide research input in production process and to study the effects of the experiment on the target viewers. While the scientific objectivity demanded that the project must be evaluated, there was also a compulsion to do so. These factors contributed a great deal in setting up of a very large communication research group in the Indian Space Research Organisation, when its leaders failed to convince the social scientists of India, about the importance of SITE and its social ramifications and implications to future satellite communications systems in India. Also SITE as the world's largest techno-social experiment laid the foundation of television research in India, which in many ways continues as a legacy of SITE (and is still some times referred to as SITE Continuity Research). The SITE research also laid the foundation for target oriented studies as its primary viewers were divided between adults and school going children in the age group of 5-12 years. Within the adult group, special target viewers like primary school teachers, village level workers, and farmers further segmented the study groups. While majority of the SITE related studies were conducted by specially selected social scientists of the Indian Space Research Organisation, some were also conducted by individuals and research institutions. SITE research followed a conceptual frame which is described in Figure 8.2. The three research traditions of anthropology, sociology and psychology were followed in SITE research. SITE was conceived and a continuing activity for Indian National Satellite (INSAT) programme rather than a terminal one. The social scientists with their discipline based theoretical orientation, collectively and sometimes independently started conducting television related studies. Their central concern was to define the cultural characteristics of television viewers, their needs and to produce research support to improve the technical and educational content of television programmes. At times the theoretical pre-occupations of the social scientists came in direct conflict with the requirements of the television producers, on other occasions it came very handy. For example, with the help of anthropologist Benedict's (1934) configurational approach the audience profiles were prepared. Around the configuration the total culture was portrayed giving a psycho-cultural picture which was needed to help producers to know their television viewers. Keeping in view the multi-linguistic characteristic of Indian television viewers, detailed linguistic analyses were also made to find out if there could be a "common" language of television acceptable to viewers of several languages. In methodological terms, most of these studies followed qualitative, descriptive field methods supported by quantitative and secondary data. It would be important to point out that such a research technique was quite close to traditional anthropological methods, generally used in rural and tribal studies. Similarly, need assessment studies followed anthropologist Goodenough (1963), while analysing viewers needs like, "felt needs", "observed needs" and "real needs". While audience profile need assessment studies were influenced by anthropological traditions, the programme pre-testing were influenced by psychological and educational traditions. The Children's Television Workshop (CTW) model of the United States of America provided the back-bone for the pre-testing of Children's Television programme and some of the adult programmes. The innovative part in these studies were related to the application of these methods in culture specific contexts. For example, testing of script in pre-production phase was followed and strongly recommended, keeping in view the linguistic hierarchy and diversity that exists within a given language in India, leave aside different languages. The assumption in doing so was that it would lead to better production, hence better effect at lower cost to achieve the educational goals. It would not be out of place to mention that this was the first time in India that any formative research was conducted on such a scale. These pretesting, later known to be as "quick and dirty" research were found very useful by the producers. The most important outcome of the SITE formative research was the beginning of the "team mode of television production". This tradition of research by and large has fairly spread in Indian television production within Doordarshan, outside Doordarshan and specially among educational institutions that make children's television programmes and programmes for higher education. There is no doubt that there is a varying degree of research involvement and commitment, but it is in no way an unknown commodity for policy-makers, producers and social researchers in India, today. However, there is a lack of serious training facility in this areas, a point that must be kept in view while discussing television studies in the Indian context.

Process Research

SITE once again provided an unique opportunity to conduct feedback studies on a regular basis. During the SITE year, the researchers lived in the villages to collect feedback data on regular basis. Given the field situation, there was no other way to collect feedback data as earlier experiences have indicated that data collected through village television custodians was unreliable. Although, a very sound research design was conceived for feedback studies, the feedback reports did not find favour with the producers. Modifications were made both in method of data collection and in presentation. As of now, no nation-wide method of feedback has been evolved on a regular basis. Though from time to time, market research organisations have started bringing out "ratings" of selected programmes after the introduction of commercial advertisements on television. Also these feedback reports have been focusing on the urban television owning families, and very little is known about rural viewers. There is a need to evolve better feedback research designs applicable to rural and urban Indian situations for different target audiences, to help producers, decision makers and policy makers.

Content analysis is considered an indirect but systematic method for observing and analysing, expressed television behaviour. During SITE and after SITE, several content analyses studies have been made. Typically, the methods evolved in the United States, have been followed in content analysis studies. Agricultural programmes were content analysed, along with several developmental programmes. However, there is not a single study where any serious efforts has been made to relate the effects and the content of the television programme. It would be desirable to develop methods and techniques of content analysis in the Indian cultural context at a national and regional level, given the linguistic multiplicity. Such an analysis will provide possible indirect effects of television on both national and regional languages and linguistic behaviour, little investigated so far. At present the microscopic minority of television viewers share an international language, English and largely spoken variant of Hindi which has not, permitted such an analysis. In the future such television studies, would be of great relevance.

Summative Research

A summative research in the Indian television to measure its effects started from its inception. During SITE intensive field work using a holistic approach in a comparative perspective to understand the process of television communication within the cultural context was conducted in nine states of India for a period of about 18 months. It had three distinct methodological advantages in providing (a) intensive first hand data, (b) a great deal of indepth and intimate understanding of the process of communication and change, and (c) descriptive analysis of the socio-cultural reality depicted as a whole—the whole being a SITE village. The theoretical assumption was that an Indian village can be conceived as a whole for such a research study. The results of these studies provided microlevel process data on village communication and the role of television in initiating change. To what extent this research method for studying television effects is useful in other Asian and African cultures need to be discussed in the culture-specific context. Keeping in view the historical development of television research, *vis-a-vis* other social sciences, the question raised here is whether there can be a research tool free from being "culture specific" allowing deeper probing and understanding of communication process *in situ* to be utilized. The psychological methods and techniques were used to measure the impact of television viewing on the school children. Broadly the study design consisted of experimental design of experimental (SITE) and control (non-SITE) school children of III and IV grades. A similar design was followed for measuring the effects of television on adult television viewers. Theoretically in all these studies, it was assumed that the information provided through television would go through a process of adoption which could be measured by using an experimental research design as done in several studies all over the world. Two major deviations in the research design in case of SITE relate to an unequal control and experimental sample sizes, and an additional observation "during" SITE in addition to pre and post observations. What are some of its methodological implications? No serious discussions have taken place among the social scientists on these issues in India and outside India.

During this period an effort to conduct television studies to measure the level of utilization in development and education was conducted along with the study of organisation and management of the television system. Generally, these studies followed the social science research approach in which the case study approach and participant observation technique was most common. These studies provided new insights into the organisation, management and the motivation aspects of projects like SITE. In a way such studies have broken new grounds for the understanding of modern operational organisations like television production and transmission. There is a need for management studies of television organisations of India and elsewhere, because its understanding would help integrate modern communication systems into the existing management structures. Television studies in India should not be considered complete without understanding the ominipresent cinema in the Indian television. Very little is known about the factors associated with the comparative preferences between cinema and television. It is a matter of common knowledge that a 'cinema show' on television is considered the most popular programme, breaking all linguistic barriers. However, we do not have much empirical evidence to know the reasons and factors associated with this popularity. Television studies will not be complete without taking this aspect of cinema into consideration. It is, therefore, suggested that future television studies must take this aspect into consideration.

Technology Leapfrog Without Research

Most of the television studies that were conceived or initiated during SITE, continued after the Indian National Satellite (INSAT) was launched and rapid expansion of television took place in India. Two significant events that occured in the process are : (1) the transmission of Hindi and English television programmes for the entire country, where more than 15 languages are spoken, each having a literary tradition of several centuries, and (2) the research studies shifted their attention from formative and process research to programme rating and programme viewing coupled with serious efforts on the part of marketing research organisations to monopolize the use of television for creating consummerism in India. These efforts have given a third dimension to television studies in India. It is no accident that in 1981, *TV Audience Survey Viewership Measurement and Reactions to Advertisements* (New Delhi; A report by Directorate General : Doordarshan) was conducted. During the same period under the pressure of the private sector the television authorities appointed a committee to rationalize the advertisement rates for television. Now the flood-gate is open and a large sum of money is being invested in television studies both for producing slick programmes to attract audience attention and to measure the effectiveness of advertisements. Of course majority of these studies are fairly obscure and out of public sight, but being carefully read by the advertising moghuls to advise their clients and to take decisions regarding television advertising investments. It would be difficult at this stage to predict whether these studies will follow the western models of television research or would there be an evolution of Indian research methods in this area.

Video has taken the Indian television viewer by storm. There is a very high ratio of video cassette recorder owning families *vis-a-vis* television in India. It has brought out another dimension for television studies in India. Some efforts have been made to study the video penetration and its effects on television viewing. Preliminary studies indicate that video viewing has curtailed television viewing time, along with cinema viewing. Few believe that the video might relegate television to second position but this needs to be studied. It is suggested that future television studies in India must include video viewing, its effects while conducting any study relating to television.

There has been a recurrent argument among the protoganists that television ostentatiously was brought to India for education and development and it must be appropriately utilized for this purpose. They have also argued that television should not become a toy of entertainment for the rich. Since 1975, it has also been pointed out that television has been used for image building. The unstated aim of television expansion was to help build images. However, very little research is available to examine this question in detail. It would be appropriate to conduct several studies to evaluate and examine to what extent, television as a medium of communication has contributed in image building and to what extent has it been used for this purpose with substantial results. These research questions gain greater importance in the light of television ownership and viewership in India and specially when there is a lukewarm and low priority given for providing public access to television in India.

Another issue which is gaining greater attention by some researchers, related to the *de facto* use of television for keeping a large proportion of India's population from making greater demand for sharing power and scarce resources. Some have reported to it as a "capitalistic conspiracy of communication". In simpler terms, the argument put forward is, that there is a conscious and planned real effort to use the medium for creating the images of chaotic social tension, conflict and violence to keep the aspiring poor to fight amongst themselves so that the rich could continue to hog the scarce resources and to centralize the power by careful manipulation of the mass media especially, visual media like cinema and television. Beyond public pronouncements, public debates and political insinuations, little research work has been done to analyse at any length, as to what is really happening to the Indian television and its viewing, and to what extent is there any substance in these pronouncements. Longitudinal studies will be needed to measure such effects, if any, which ought to be done in India and other countries. If television is creating an information gap between the poor and the rich it ought to be a national concern, as an equal access to information for the functioning of a democratic country is a necessary condition and it ought to be ensured.

REFERENCES

Agrawal, Binod C. (1976 a). SITE Social Evaluation : An Expose. *In SITE Winter School.* January 16-28, 1976, Ahmedabad, Space Applications Centre.

Agrawal, Binod C. (1977 b). Satellite Instructional Television Experiment : A Social Evaluation. In *Evaluating Educational Television and Radio*, Tony Bates and John Robinson (eds). Milton Keynes : The Open University Press.

Agrawal, Binod C. (1981). SITE Social Evaluation : Results Experiences and Implications. Ahmedabad : Space Applications Centre.

Benedict, Ruth F. (1934). *Patterns of Culture.* New York : Houghton Mifflin.

Goodenough, Ward H. (1963). *Cooperation in Change.* New York : Russell Sage Foundation.

Neurath, Paul (ed). "School Television in Delhi". All-India Radio, New Delhi.

Rogers, E.M. (1962). *Diffusion of Innovations.* New York : The Free Press.

INDEX